"I've had the pleasure of know. twenty years. I consider Bart a true professional who is at the very top of his field. The concepts that Bart teaches will serve both the consumer and the insurance agent alike. Learn Bart's philosophy about how to be properly covered and protect your assets and your family. This book is a must-read."

TROY KORSGADEN
President, Korsgaden International

"Everyone that owns a home, automobile, or personal property must read this book. Well, now that I think about it, anyone alive must read this book and use it as a guide to protect themselves and their loved ones. The Gap Elimination Checklist that Bart provides at the end of each chapter is an excellent checklist and empowers readers to ask their insurance brokers some well-informed questions prior to buying or renewing insurance. A relevant and compelling read. I wish I read it ten years ago!"

REGGIE CHANDRA, PhD, PE
Founder and CEO, Rhythm Engineering

"In my thirty-plus years of working in the real estate and financial world, I have come across many different types of people. Many of them make professional promises they cannot keep, or say something and do the opposite. Bart Baker is not one of those people. I can always count on him to get the job done when and how I want it. He is very knowledgeable in his field, and I know he is always offering me the best service that he can find. Bart always has your best interest in mind. With the future of the economic climate unknown, it is good to know that you can count on having the right insurance should emergencies arise. I love working with Bart, and hope to continue to do so for as long as I can."

KOUROSH AKHTARZAD
President, Nasa Management

"As a financial advisor specializing in working with high-income, high-net-worth business owners since 1989, I have seen the concepts Bart Baker writes about in real life: both the happy stories, and the not-so-happy stories. Fortunately, the happy stories had an insurance broker like Bart attached who cared, who had a relationship with his customer, and who implemented the type of insurance needed.

Bart goes one step further. He shows all of us how important that relationship is, and empowers us to better find a solid relationship with the right broker for us. He does this through demystifying a world most people don't want to deal with: insurance. Most don't want to because they don't understand it, and therefore feel inadequate. Simplifying the complex, Bart helps all of us be better insurance consumers and protect our assets, our loved ones, and our livelihoods.

I consider this book a must-read for all my business-owner clients."

STEVE BEATTY
President, Financial Solutions for Business

If an **Elephant Sits on You, Are You Covered?**

*How to Talk with Your Insurance Agent
to Be Properly Insured*

Bart Baker, LUTCF

Think It Publishing

Malibu, California

If an Elephant Sits on You, Are You Covered?
How to Talk with Your Insurance Agent to be Properly Insured

Bart Baker

Published by Think It Publishing, Malibu, California, USA
Copyright © 2014 by Bart Baker
All rights reserved.

Think It Publishing
29169 Heathercliff Road, Suite 208
Malibu, CA 90265-4183
(310) 457-5092
bart@bwbaker.com

Limit of Liability/Disclaimer of Warranty:

Publishing manager: Helen Chang, www.authorbridgemedia.com
Editor: Kristine Serio, www.authorbridgemedia.com
Publishing assistant: Carla Baker
Cover and Interior design: Peri Poloni-Gabriel, www.knockoutbooks.com

Library of Congress Control Number: 2014936533

ISBN: 978-0-9960552-0-8
ISBN (hardcover): 978-0-9960552-1-5
ISBN: (e-book): 978-0-9960552-2-2

Ordering information:
Quantity sales. Special discounts are available on quantity purchases by corporations, associations, and others. For details, contact the publisher at the address above.

Printed in the United States of America

Dedication

To my amazing, loving family: my wife, Wendy;
my children, Jaime, Amber, and Brian; my sons-in-law, Jason
and Fabian; my grandchildren, Jake, Jonah, Julian, and Luca;
my mother, Elaine; my mother-in-law, Norma; my brother,
Ben; and my late brother, Beau.

A special dedication to my father, who left far too early in life.
I aspire to uphold the standards you set for us all.

You have all made me a happy man.

⟨∞⟩

Table of Contents

Acknowledgments

I t's been said that no man is an island, and this couldn't be truer than it is in my case. I have been blessed with the most amazing people who have provided support and encouragement to me every step of the way in the creation of this book and in my life.

As in most things in my life, I have to start with my wife and partner, Wendy. I don't think it's possible to find more support and encouragement than what you provide to me. Thank you for everything.

I owe my success to my incredible team at BW Baker Insurance. My staff has been with me for years and "gets" what we need to do to keep a customer happy and satisfied. A very special thanks to Maria, Michelle, Flo, George, Kim, Virginia, Griselda, Dulce, Bianca, and Kyle. An extra-special note of appreciation goes out to my assistant, Vanessa, for helping to keep me on track, even when I added this project to her already busy workload.

Thank you to my business coaches at Strategic Coach, Adrienne Duffy and Dan Sullivan. The tools and concepts that you teach, along with all the support you provide, have made a huge difference in my life.

Whenever I needed confirmation that I was on the right track, I was able to reach out to good friends and fellow insurance brokers like Stacy Korsgaden, Shelley Liu, Yannick Truchi, and Jessie Navarro. Their help and dedication to this business have been steadfast. I appreciate all that you do!

Thank you to Charley Beals, my good friend, district manager, sounding board, and advisor. Your incredible support over the years has made a huge difference in my life.

My thanks also to Craig Bass for always pushing me to see myself as being larger than I am. You are a truly wonderful teacher and coach in this business. Your agents are lucky to have you.

To Helen Chang and her talented team at Author Bridge Media: you have been a joy to work with and have been instrumental in bringing this book to fruition. You turned what seemed to be an almost overwhelming project into a reality. Thank you for your great support and professionalism!

Thank you to Peri Poloni-Gabriel of Knockout Design for your creative vision and design talents. Your artistic guidance has been invaluable, and I am extremely thankful for your excellent work.

Carla Baker, your endless direct support and work on this book have made everything better. Thank you for joining the team. I appreciate it.

My friends and clients Sam and Gail Seelig, as well as Jerry and Patty Seymour, have been invaluable. Thank you for assuring me that I was on the right track when it came to communicating with customers. Your friendship, support, and time are valued more than you know.

Bill Elliott, you have been extremely valuable in discussing the concepts in this book, and in helping to keep its contents as simple as possible. Your depth of knowledge of this business knows no bounds. Thank you for sharing it with me.

To my mentor AC Warnack, you are the finest example of character, integrity, and business acumen that I have ever had the pleasure to meet. Your friendship means the world to me. Thank you for your guidance.

Finally, thank you to Scott Lindquist for your unwavering support and feedback. You have played a great role in my growth by helping to clear the way for my success. You know how to get things done, and your insight, direction, and support are sincerely appreciated.

Introduction

Change is not merely necessary to life, it is life.

—ALVIN TOFFLER

Saving Lives

People often ask me, "How can you be passionate about something like insurance?"

I wasn't always an insurance agent. My earlier career was in firefighting with the Los Angeles County Fire Department. I spent twenty years protecting homes, inspecting properties, working car accidents, responding to medical emergencies, and seeing more untimely deaths than I could have ever imagined.

I was a good fireman and loved the job, but one day, when I was on patrol in Malibu doing brush inspections, a call came in about a man having a heart attack. Being the closest responder, I was the first on the scene.

A woman greeted me at the front door of a beautiful house, and she looked scared to death. She said, "My husband, my husband!" and led me into her first-floor bedroom, where he was lying face up on top of their bed.

He was sweating and pale. I checked his airway, and he wasn't breathing. Then I looked for a pulse and did not find one. That told me I had to start CPR. The bed was high and soft, and you just can't do CPR on a bed like that; you need to have a firm surface.

He was a very large man, and his wife couldn't help me, so I pulled him off the bed by myself. While I was doing that, I felt a sharp pain in my back. I ignored it that day because there was so much going on, but my back started bothering me all the time after that. I later found that I had herniated a disc, which started a downhill spiral. Firefighting is a physical job, and it got to the point where I couldn't do it anymore. In the end, it started a journey to other opportunities, which led me to the insurance business.

Today I'm still protecting people, but in a different way. My career as a fireman led to my passion for insurance. I think it has to do with seeing all of that death and destruction. I put out fires and handled medical incidents, but the aftermath was intense. I found that the greatest product ever invented is waiting in the wings to put people's lives back together. That discovery changed the direction of my life.

As great a product as insurance is, though, it's like a meal at a restaurant. You can have a mediocre dining experience or a memorable meal that you tell your friends about. This book is written to help you learn more about insurance and explore thoroughly what it means to be a properly insured individual or family. I hope that when you finish reading this book, you'll feel certain that you either have, or will be on your way to having, a fortress around your assets that no outside force can destroy.

Developing Your Philosophy

Have you noticed that all successful people have a philosophy that drives them? The right philosophy is like a compass pointing north. If you get off track, it's your personal philosophy that allows you to self-correct, get back on track, and make decisions with ease. The goal of this book is to give you the information you need to form your own philosophy about insurance. When you are presented with various options for coverage, the right choices will jump out at you.

Throughout this book, I'll share anecdotes with and without examples of proper coverage. As you read them, picture yourself in these situations and realize that you have the power to do something. All you need to do is act proactively.

The purpose of this book is not to make you an insurance expert in one sitting. It is to educate you and give you the tools you need to have an informed conversation with your insurance professional so that you understand what endorsements are available and how they will apply to you. Knowledge is power, and by the time you're done reading this book, your knowledge will have increased, along with your understanding of what is important in the world of insurance and why.

With the help of this book, you'll learn how to develop your guiding philosophy. You'll learn which steps to take to find the right coverage for your unique needs—for your home, your car, your life, and more. The good part is that you don't have to do this on your own. You'll work with an insurance professional who will assist in creating and maintaining the right plan for you. If you have such a person now, that's terrific! This book will help you have a deeper dialogue with that person. If you don't have such a relationship, we'll discuss how to find the right fit for you. Either way, your knowledge and awareness are going to increase immensely.

The Gap Elimination Process™

Over the last twenty-five years, I've developed my own philosophy about insurance that has been honed through working on thousands of claims. I can say with absolute certainty that there is a way to be properly insured, and in this book, I will teach you that way.

I call it The Gap Elimination Process™. You can apply this system to either a family or an individual insurance program so that the right coverage is used and gaps are eliminated. That means you won't have too much or too little coverage. It's important to eliminate redundancies and get the best cost and value. You want to make sure all available discounts are applied.

I will walk you through each insurance product so that you have a clear understanding of the different types of coverage. I will also discuss how to properly apply The Gap Elimination Process™ for a particular type of coverage. I want you to feel confident that you are getting the best insurance and that your assets are protected.

At the end of each chapter is a checklist designed for each policy type, such as home, auto, umbrella, life, disability, long-term care, earthquake, and flood. The checklist will show the available features and endorsements. It will also provide the meaning of each coverage component and explain how it may relate to you.

Our lives are dynamic and ever-changing, so a review process needs to be established to ensure that The Gap Elimination Process™ remains relevant. Some people need to review their policies more frequently. The more you have to insure and the more dynamic your lifestyle, the more you need to review your coverage. It should be like doing taxes once a year or going for an annual physical examination, because insurance coverage is that important. You need to check in at least once a year and make sure that everything is covered correctly. These meetings are when you'll apply your proactive philosophy.

Importance of Participation

I have clients who are doctors, lawyers, and business owners who don't understand insurance at all. They want me to just handle it for them. I appreciate the compliment, but it's about *your* life and *your* possessions. A basic understanding can take you a long way. Getting insurance is a participatory process. You wouldn't have a medical procedure without knowing the potential side effects so that you can weigh the risks and rewards. The same principle applies to insurance.

Insurance is a way to help put your life back in order. It's worth paying the additional premium for certain coverage because insurance doesn't really cost—insurance pays. It creates a secure fortress around you. However, if you're not covered correctly, then insurance does cost you because it's not going to pay you correctly. You can choose to be fully covered, minimally covered, or something in between.

If you compare the process to buying a car, you can get something providing basic transportation that may not be very reliable or spend more and get new transportation that's reliable, or do even better and buy something that is reliable, comfortable, and perhaps a little luxurious. Once you decide what type of experience you prefer for you and your family, your insurance broker can help to create the right plan. The final decision is ultimately yours.

Plan Ahead

It's vital to plan your insurance properly before a crisis happens. Sadly, that Malibu man who had a heart attack ended up dying. I couldn't save him.

Then something amazing happened. I got a call one day from a woman who said she'd like to talk about insuring her home. As I drove up to her house, I thought, "My God, I know this house." I went in and found it was the same woman. I told her that I was the fireman on the scene when her husband died. It was an emotional meeting.

I hadn't been there to help her get the right amount of life insurance coverage they needed for her husband. I don't know what they had. But she became my client for many years, and I made sure that her home, cars, and everything else were insured properly. I take a lot of pride in that.

∽

I can think of no more stirring symbol of man's humanity to man than a fire engine.

—**KURT VONNEGUT**

Chapter 1

Investing in Your Life

Life is inherently risky. There is only one big risk you should avoid at all costs, and that is the risk of doing nothing.

—DENIS WAITLEY

Safari

A few years ago, my wife's girlfriend and her husband were on a safari. They were taking photos of a herd of elephants. The husband got a little too close and perhaps a little complacent. As he reached up to take the perfect shot, the elephant raised its body and sat on him. In the flash of a camera, his life was gone.

This was a tragic ending. He was not my client, and I'm not sure if he had life insurance. But his wife was devastated. Her life was altered forever.

When something seriously wrong happens in your life, it can feel like the weight of the world is on you—heavy, like an elephant sitting on you. As you read this book, my goal is for you to implement the suggestions and strategies shared within these pages so that you never feel the weight, and if you do, it is for the shortest time possible.

The visual you can take from this is to avoid the elephant. When structuring your insurance portfolio, make sure that the walls are high. The good news is that you will not do it alone. You can work with a professional, and by reading this book, you'll have a clear understanding of what's important.

The Importance of Being Properly Insured

Being properly insured is one of the most important things you can do; otherwise, the consequences can be incredibly dire. The interesting thing about insurance is that after you actually know that you need it, you can't get it. In other words, underwriters can't offer you coverage if they see a looming claim on the horizon.

Consider it an investment in your life. If you were told that you only had six months left to live, how much life insurance would you want to get for your family? The answer, of course, is as much as you possibly can, but the reality is that you're not going to be able to get any. Insurance—especially life insurance—has to be proactively approached, because the moment you know you have a potential need, only the decisions you made proactively will be able to back you up.

Falling $450,000 Short

A few years ago, a home in my neighborhood was destroyed in a fire. I heard that the owner had to pay $450,000 out of pocket to rebuild because he didn't have enough building ordinance coverage. Building ordinance pays for the increased cost of construction due to building code changes.

His policy provided $50,000 of building ordinance coverage. The actual cost to bring the home up to current building code standards was $500,000, so he was $450,000 short.

It's possible that he told his agent to get a home policy and never looked at the features. He didn't know what he didn't know, and it cost him a lot of money.

Have a Conversation

You should have an understanding of how each policy benefits you. Later on, I'll break down each type of policy and explain everything that is covered, what things are typically overlooked, and why those things are important.

When you look at the coverage you currently have or when you're having a new discussion, you want to understand what is and is not being said. I've heard people say many times that the amount of coverage in their homeowners policy was the same as what they paid for their house. Homeowners insurance has very little to do with the actual cost paid for your home.

Many other aspects of homeowners insurance need to be discussed in order to ensure that a home is properly taken care of, as we'll see in the chapter on homeowners insurance. That's why it's so important to discuss the details of your policy with your broker.

Don't Let Your Agent Choose for You

I want to reiterate how important it is to be an active participant in your insurance decisions. Insurance carriers can provide concierge-type services that rival what you would experience at a fine hotel. A good insurance broker has the ability to match you with the right carriers to get the service experience and professionalism that you want. We can show you how to change deductibles and free up dollars when you need them.

But there are all kinds of agents out there. When people come to my office with their homeowners policy, I ask them who came up with the coverage limits. Why is their three-thousand-square-foot house insured for $350,000? They don't know. They tell me it's what their agent chose.

Don't leave these types of decisions to somebody else! You don't know who has your best interests at heart. It's possible that the agent was only trying to find you the cheapest possible price, but we all know that the cheapest isn't always the right solution.

Get to know the agent you're dealing with, and make sure you trust that person from the beginning. Your agent may be a great, honest person with your best interests at heart; however, this isn't true of everyone who has a license to sell insurance. At the end of the day, it's your home and your assets on the line. Your insurance philosophy will guide you in making the right decisions, with the help of our checklist of items to discuss with your agent.

As an agent, I appreciate your confidence in me. However, we still need to have a conversation. You need to participate in this process. It's not boring! And wouldn't you rather make sure that we are on the same page? If something bad does occur, you will be able to pick up the phone, tell your agent what happened, and have the issue handled and resolved.

Have More Than "Some Insurance"

It's easy to say you're insured, but you are only truly insured when you can be made whole after a crisis. You have "some insurance" when a carrier participates by giving you some money, but you've got to come up with the rest of it yourself to put your life back together again.

The claim experience should be simple. Whether a claim is for a fender bender or the loss of a home and its contents, my staff and I make sure that our clients are well taken care of throughout the claims process. Our ability to comfort you and your family with this response is the product of a process that was started with a simple conversation using our Gap Elimination Process™.

Believers and Skeptics

After twenty-five-plus years of being in this business, I have found that there are two types of people when it comes to insurance: believers and skeptics. Believers are people who want to be properly insured. Skeptics think nothing will happen to them and want to cut their coverage to the bone. They often don't even consider the concept of having all of their assets protected. This book is written for the first group; the people who want to protect their homes, families, and lives.

I frequently find that people in the second group become believers as soon as they're faced with a life-changing event and are unable to pick up the phone and have it handled. That is a very expensive education.

The benefit to a better understanding of your policy is that you get properly covered. You don't have to wonder and worry about what will happen if your house burns down. You will have done the work and research in advance, and you will have confidence that your home will be secure.

Chapter 2

Homeowners Insurance

A man travels the world over in search of what he needs and returns home to find it.

—GEORGE AUGUSTUS MOORE

Home Sweet Home

For several years, while I was transitioning from a firefighter to an insurance agent, I worked both jobs simultaneously. Until I hurt my back, I had always seen disasters through the eyes of the fire department. Terrible things happened, and it was a shame, but I only stayed long enough to stanch the bleeding. I was never involved in the aftermath.

Then the Malibu fires of 1993 came raging through the area when I was on the engine company. It was the largest blaze I had ever been assigned to. More than five hundred homes were destroyed. It was like a war zone. Afterward, my crew and I drove through the ravaged neighborhoods, viewing the awful destruction. As we turned down a street where all the houses had burned to the ground, we passed a plot that I had visited before.

The home that had stood there belonged to one of my clients, a wonderful woman named Gretchen. As I stared at that blackened patch of earth, I realized that I actually had the power to do something about it. I *had* to do something about this.

For the first time, I was going to work on both sides of the disaster to put lives back together again.

The next day, after I got off duty, I changed out of my fireman's clothes into a nice suit and tie, and called my adjustor. I was both nervous and excited as I drove him to the site where Gretchen's house had been. The air was heavy with smoke, and the cement beneath our feet was still hot as we walked around and surveyed the damage. Then we headed down to Malibu Pier, where the adjustor had set up a temporary office in a construction trailer.

"Do you have the policy?" he asked.

I did. This was before the days of the Internet and electronic documents. I set the folder down in front of him, and we reviewed the policy. Then he nodded, opened his checkbook, and started writing out checks. I was amazed. He gave me hundreds of thousands of dollars for Gretchen's home, on the spot. Then we filed the claim and got the remaining balance paid in full before Gretchen had even talked to me.

That experience changed my perspective on my new career. On Friday, I had been a fireman. On Saturday, I was an insurance broker. Both jobs had been critical to getting Gretchen's life back on track as quickly as possible. Some people on her street spent years battling it out with their insurance companies to begin the rebuilding process, but Gretchen's claim was settled in a couple of days, and reconstruction on her home began right away because I had made sure that she was covered properly. For the first time, I understood the true value of being properly insured. It was an incredible feeling.

The Basics of Homeowners Insurance

Apart from the people you love most in the world, your home is the rock that you build the rest of your life around. It is a center of security and stability. When you have a bad day at work, just the thought of getting home and collapsing into your favorite armchair can be comforting. You count on your house to be dependable, and having a strong homeowners insurance policy is a key part of the dependability equation. If you have the right homeowners insurance, you will be protected from the "elephant" of a disaster at home.

The concept of homeowners insurance was conceived by statesman and scientist Benjamin Franklin, who helped form the first firefighting organization in Philadelphia in 1736 following a disastrous fire. His idea was to have a club that men could join to help one another save their homes and businesses in the event of fire. Each member was required to own two leather buckets, attend a monthly meeting to discuss recent fires, and train to fight future ones. Members who missed a meeting were fined, and the money went toward buying additional equipment.

Franklin's organization became so popular that similar clubs began to sprout up all over the city. Before long, the mutual aid program—in which neighboring fire departments helped each other in times of need—was formed. This program is still around today. Franklin's next step was to form The Philadelphia Contributionship in 1752, the nation's first successful fire insurance company. Members were required to take out a seven-year policy, at the end of which the premium was returned to the member who had paid it, minus claims and expenses.

Today, homeowners insurance covers much more than fire. It can include earthquakes, water damage, theft, wind, personal property, separate structures (any structure that is not attached to your home, such as a pool, guest house, garage, or fence), landscape, backup of sewer drains, liability, and workers' compensation, to name a few. With many moving parts, more things can go wrong with a homeowners policy than with any other type of insurance coverage. If you only focus on the amount of coverage you want for the structure itself, you will miss a huge part of the other items that you need to pay attention to.

I knew a woman who employed a gardener for yard work. While doing some pruning, the man fell out of one of her trees and broke his neck. He sued her because the accident happened on her property. In another case, a gardener was mowing the grass when he tripped on a rock, and his boot went under the mower. He lost his foot, and that was another lawsuit. Both homeowners had insurance on their houses, but neither had thought of purchasing coverage for workers' compensation. That doesn't usually come up when you're discussing policies with your agent.

Most home policies come with workers' comp for part-time household employees like maids and gardeners. The number of hours worked per week by part-time employees is typically defined as up to twenty. If your household employee works more than that, you should have your broker endorse the policy for a full-time position. It doesn't cost much, and it will be the difference between a claim being covered or not. Don't assume you have workers' comp—ask your broker.

A house is usually a person's biggest asset, so you don't want to roll the dice when it comes to making sure that it's properly covered. Risk transfer should be the primary goal in home insurance, and it is usually possible to achieve that 100 percent. Still, occasionally an insurance carrier may resist. Maybe you have an older home in an area where building ordinance laws have changed a lot over the years. In that case, the insurance carrier may not want to offer you full building ordinance coverage. Even in those situations, however, it is usually possible to hedge the issue in question. It is always better to be aware of what your policy does and does not cover.

Gap Elimination Checklist

Everyone has homeowners insurance, but not everyone knows the difference between a policy that will really take care of you when disaster strikes and one that leaves you in financial devastation after a loss. When you look at the coverage you have or when you have a discussion about new coverage, you want to understand what is being said and not said.

Use the following checklist to begin The Gap Elimination Process™ discussion for homeowners insurance with your agent. During the meeting, make sure that every item is covered and that you have a thorough understanding of each.

✓ **Actual Cash Value:** The cost of replacing damaged or destroyed property with comparable new property. The actual cash value is calculated minus depreciation, but is limited by the maximum dollar amount shown on the declarations page of your policy. Most policies replace things based on replacement cost rather than strict actual cash value. Whenever possible, get a replacement cost policy.

✓ **Replacement Cost:** The dollar amount needed to replace damaged personal property or dwelling property without deducting for depreciation. Your replacement cost is limited by the maximum dollar amount shown on the declarations page of your policy.

✓ **Backup of Sewer and Drains**: Have you ever heard of your drains flowing the wrong way? They can, and when it happens, it's never pretty. Know how much coverage you have in the event of backed-up drains and sewers. If the default amount is low and makes you uneasy, you have the option of increasing it until you are comfortable.

✓ **Building Ordinance (BO)**: Building ordinance coverage, which is particularly critical in older homes, is probably one of the most important and overlooked parts of a home policy. This endorsement pays for the increased cost of construction due to building code changes. If your home were to be damaged to the extent that the building department required you to comply with new building ordinances during reconstruction, your home policy would not cover those added costs by default. It would only pay to rebuild exactly what you had before, even if what you had wasn't up to the current code. The amount of compensation that is allocated toward complying with the newest building ordinances is only determined by how much building ordinance coverage you have, specifically.

For example, say your home is supported by wood pilings, and the entire structure burns down in a fire. When you go to rebuild, you learn that the building ordinance code in your community no longer allows homes to be built on wood pilings. Instead, it now requires concrete pilings to be drilled into the bedrock. Concrete pilings are much more expensive than wood pilings; however, your insurance will not cover that difference unless you have a building ordinance endorsement on your policy. Know how much building ordinance coverage you need before you sign up for homeowners insurance, and get the right amount if you can.

✓ **Business on Premise:** Any type of business you conduct at home is typically excluded from your regular homeowners policy. Depending on what you do, you may want to add this endorsement to your coverage. I've heard of carriers denying slip-and-fall claims for delivery people if the injured person was delivering something for a business. Childcare is another example of an overlooked business on premises that would do well to have an endorsement. This coverage is not expensive, and like liability, it can make a huge difference when a lawsuit is filed against you.

✓ **Carrier:** You should know who your carrier is. A carrier is the company that writes your policies. Do your research before you sign up with a carrier. What is its A.M. Best rating? Is it financially secure? Is it admitted or non-admitted? A non-admitted carrier does not participate in the State Guaranty Fund. If a carrier goes out of business, the state fund will pay claims of up to $500,000. It's similar to FDIC (Federal Deposit Insurance Corporation) coverage for banks. If you do business with a strong carrier, this is usually not an issue. Keep in mind that being non-admitted is not necessarily a bad thing. Talk to your agent about differences you should be aware of if your carrier is non-admitted.

✓ **Dwelling Coverage:** How much is your house insured for? Is it enough to put you back where you are in the event of a major disaster? How was the dwelling coverage limit determined when you signed up for it?

✓ **Earthquake:** Earthquake is defined as a sudden and violent shaking of the ground, sometimes causing great destruction, as a result of movements within the earth's crust or volcanic action. Along with floods, earthquakes are excluded from the vast majority of home policies unless expressly stated otherwise. Earthquake policies are much more limited in terms of coverage than regular home policies are, and they usually come with large deductible options. Still, even though you may share in some of the costs of putting your home back together after an earthquake occurs, it is far better to have some coverage than no coverage. We will discuss both flood and earthquake insurance in more detail in chapter 8.

✓ **Extended Replacement Cost (ERC):** Determining how much coverage you need for your home is actually more of an educated guess than an exact science. Extended replacement cost, or ERC, was created in response to that. Opting into an ERC endorsement provides an additional percentage above and beyond the amount shown for your dwelling in case that fixed number is not enough to completely rebuild. ERC percentages are typically offered at 25, 50 and 100 percent of the amount of dwelling coverage. For example, if your house (structure) was insured for $1 million and you had purchased a 25 percent ERC endorsement on it, you would have up to $1.25 million to rebuild your house. Note that building ordinance costs are in addition to this limit.

✓ **Flood:** Like earthquake, the vast majority of home policies exclude flood damage. Flood is defined as rising waters from the outside that inundate two or more parcels. Tidal waters are also a part of flood damage. If you are at possible risk for flooding, you should look into getting flood insurance. Most lenders require you to purchase flood insurance if your home is in a flood zone. Your agent can help you determine whether flood insurance is a necessary part of your coverage.

✓ **Landscape:** A standard home policy usually insures your landscape at a fixed percentage of the coverage you have on your dwelling. However, a carrier often has limitations on how much it will pay for any one plant or tree. For example, a $1 million home might have $50,000 of coverage for landscaping, with a $750 maximum for any one plant or tree. If your garden is substantial, look into this. I have several clients who have insured their trees for replacement in case of a fire or some other unforeseen misfortune. Their forty-foot sycamore is worth more than my first car! Keep in mind that when purchasing landscape coverage, you will have a limit per tree or shrub and an aggregate amount to consider.

✓ **Liability:** This coverage is broader than most people realize, but you still need to make sure that you have the right endorsement. Check if you are covered for personal injury and workers' compensation. Most policies already include workers' comp for part-time maids and gardeners, but if this isn't specifically stated in your policy, then you have no coverage. Tell your insurance broker as well if you need coverage for full-time help, such as assistants, nannies, cooks, and care providers. This cost is reasonable, and the penalties can be crippling if someone sues you and you don't have liability coverage.

✓ **Loss of Use:** If you need to move out of your home while it's being repaired after a covered claim for something like water damage or a fire, you will need a place to stay. Loss of use covers the cost of renting comparable housing. The vast majority of carriers have limits on how much and how long they'll pay for this. In some areas it takes a long time to rebuild, especially if there are multiple losses in a small region. Also keep in mind that if you have a mortgage on your home, you will still be required to pay the monthly amount. With loss-of-use coverage, you won't be out of pocket for two housing expenses while reconstruction is happening.

✓ **Mold:** Mold is the new asbestos. No one in the insurance world wants to cover it, and most carriers will only give you minimal coverage for mold damage in a standard policy. As with most aspects of homeowners insurance, know what the limitations are ahead of time. You may have the option of buying additional coverage for an extra premium.

✓ **Personal Injury:** Personal injury refers to injury other than bodily injury arising from one or more of the following offenses: false arrest, detention, or imprisonment; malicious prosecution of, wrongful entry into, or invasion of the right of private occupancy of a room, dwelling, or premises that a person occupies when committed by or on behalf of its owner, landlord, or lessor; oral or written publication of material that slanders or libels a person or organization or disparages a person's or organization's goods, products, or services; oral or written publication of material that violates a person's right of privacy.

✓ **Personal Property:** The personal property endorsement insures common items within your home, such as clothes, furnishings, and electronics. This is typically an automatic percentage of what your dwelling itself is insured for. You can increase the amount of your personal property endorsement if you want to. In most cases, however, there is no savings if you choose to decrease this coverage.

✓ **Policy Form:** Policy forms dictate how a claim is adjusted for your home or its contents. There are several different kinds of policy forms. In addition to actual cash value and replacement cost (see above), they include basic form, broad form, and special form.

    ☐ **Basic Form:** Basic form, as the name suggests, is the least comprehensive of the three options. The important thing to note about basic form policies is that they cover only *named perils*. This means that *if a coverage is not specifically named in the policy, there is no coverage.* This policy tends to be quite limited in scope and should be used with care. The types of coverage included in a typical basic form policy are:

- Fire

- Lightning

- Windstorm or hail

- Explosion

- Smoke

- Vandalism

- Aircraft or vehicle collision

- Riot or civil commotion

- Sinkhole collapse

- Volcanic activity

☐ **Broad Form:** Broad form coverage is more expansive than basic form coverage. It includes coverage for all of the hazards included in a basic form policy, plus several additional hazards that are expressly named. As with a basic form policy, a broad form policy covers only *named perils*. Again, *if a coverage is not specifically named in the policy, that coverage is excluded.* Fortunately, the broad form is designed to cover the most common forms of property damage. Coverage in a typical broad form policy (in addition to what's covered by the basic form) includes:

- Burglary/break-in damage

- Falling objects (like tree limbs)

- Freezing of plumbing

- Accidental water damage

- Artificially generated electricity

☐ **Special Form:** When a property policy is written on a special form, the insurance company has a duty to specifically exclude coverage. Simply put, if the insurance company does not exclude coverage in writing, the damage to your property will be paid for. There are a huge amount of common exclusions, including: government action, nuclear hazard, war and military action, water damage (i.e., flood), fungus, and pollution. At the end of the day, however, the special form gives you much more comprehensive insurance protection than the basic or broad forms.

✓ **Renting Out Your Home:** If you rent or are considering renting out your home for either a short or long period of time, talk to your agent about coverage. Most policies have some type of exclusion for renting. It's always a good idea to have written into the lease that the renter will provide evidence of a renter's policy. The coverage should include liability, and the owner should be named in the clause as an additional insured. This provides another layer of coverage for the owner. Regardless, always find out the details and exclusions of your homeowners policy before you decide to rent. If you rent out a home on a long-term basis, be sure to get a landlord policy.

✓ **Scheduled Items:** Although much of your personal property is covered by the personal property endorsement, most home policies have limitations for what they call "target items." These are uncommon objects such as jewelry, fine art, silverware, oriental rugs, collectible cards, comic books, money, and securities. The list can be extensive, and it's important to know what your policy limits are up front so that you can buy additional coverage if needed. It is worth taking the time to schedule your valuable jewelry and fine art. Be sure to get a stated value endorsement when you do this, so that in the event of a loss you'll be compensated for the amount that was originally stated. Some carriers will even pay an additional percentage above the original statement, if you choose carefully. We will go into scheduled items in more detail in chapter 9.

✓ **Separate Structures:** Your home insurance does not always include structures that are not attached to your home. These exceptions are covered under "separate structures" and may include things such as pools, sheds, barns, and so forth. Your policy will list an amount for separate structures. Please make sure it is enough.

✓ **Trusts:** More and more in recent years, people have chosen to title their homes in trusts and LLCs (limited liability companies) for estate tax planning and asset protection purposes. If your home is titled in anything other than your own name, be sure to tell your agent. Your agent can then amend your policy to include the entity, ensuring that coverage is provided for the trust or LLC.

☜꧁꧂☞

The happiest moments of my life have been the few which I have passed at home in the bosom of my family.

—**THOMAS JEFFERSON**

Chapter 3

Auto Insurance

Every choice you make has an end result.

—ZIG ZIGLAR

The Unlucky Jogger

Auto insurance can have more flexibility than many people realize. One such case applied to a man in Ventura County, California. He was running along the highway near the beach early one summer Saturday morning. It was around 7 a.m., and he was jogging in the wide bike lane; something he had done hundreds of times before. That day, however, his routine took a sharp turn for the worse when a distracted driver swerved on the road and hit him from behind.

He recalls feeling a sensation like flying. After that, the next thing he remembers is waking up in a hospital bed with his family gathered around him, telling him that he had been hit by a car. He had multiple broken bones in addition to internal injuries.

The man owned his own business, and he was very hands-on in running it. After the accident, he couldn't manage things as before. The driver who hit him only had a $15,000 minimum liability policy and no assets. In some cases, that might have been really bad news. But this particular man happened to have $250,000 of uninsured motorist, plus umbrella coverage with uninsured motorist on it.

When the compensation he received from the reckless driver's insurance wasn't enough to get him through the recovery process, his own policy stepped in and covered the rest. Although he wasn't even in a car when the accident happened, his auto insurance came through for him. He avoided the financial "elephant" of the auto disaster.

The Basics of Auto Insurance

Driving is something that most of us take for granted. It's become such a routine part of our lives that we sometimes forget to consider the risk involved every time we get into a car. Each year in the United States, about 30,000 people die in automobile collisions, and an additional 2.35 million people are injured or disabled. Plenty of people are afraid of flying, but in reality driving is the more dangerous form of transportation.

Your car is one of your largest areas of exposure to liability. Over the years, my office has had thousands of claims. By far, the ones with the largest liability have come from car accidents. You may think of yourself as a safe driver, but there's a lot more to it. Maybe you have inexperienced teenagers learning how to drive in your vehicle. Maybe you leave your car with the valet parking attendant now and then. Who knows if that attendant has coverage or how good it is if he or she does have it? Then there are friends and family members. How many of them borrow your car once in a while or offer to drive home if that second glass of pinot noir from your favorite Italian restaurant makes you a little too relaxed to take the wheel yourself?

The point is that even if you are the best driver out there, the liability exposure to you in every one of those situations is 100 percent, because you own the car. Anything that happens involving your car comes back to impact you at the end of the day, no matter who was driving.

Cheap rates for auto insurance may be tempting, but always make sure you know what you're getting before you sign up. For example, some carriers with cheap rates have a named driver policy, meaning that coverage will only apply if one of the people named on the policy is driving at the time of the claim. In another "gotcha," some cheap carriers will say you're covered regardless of who is driving, but will then drop the amount of coverage to $15,000 if the driver in question is not named on the policy. In other words, you get what you pay for. You want your policy to allow coverage for permissive-use drivers.

Carriers can deny auto insurance claims if the residents of a household are not disclosed. Let's say Mr. and Mrs. Jones have a seventeen-year-old son, and they haven't notified their carrier that Johnny has a license now and drives one of their cars. The carrier can and usually does deny coverage if it receives a claim involving the undisclosed driver. Again, this is a huge liability exposure and is never worth potential savings on premiums.

Young Drivers

Young drivers are expensive to insure—and rightfully so. The number of claims filed by this group of drivers is dramatically more than that of experienced drivers.

That said, you may be able to persuade carriers to lower their rates for your teenaged driver. For instance, most carriers have a good student discount that goes into effect when the student driver maintains a grade point average of B or better. Some carriers also have an online course that a teen can take in order to take advantage of a large discount. Or get your teenager's first car thinking that it's a training car, so if it's totaled, it's totaled. Then opt out of collision coverage, which is very expensive for young drivers.

My son's first car was a used Chevrolet pickup truck. A few days after taking over the keys, he went to visit a friend and parked the truck in front of the friend's garage door. Later, as he was leaving, he accidentally put the gear in reverse instead of drive and backed the truck straight through the garage door. I was glad I had good insurance!

One final thing to consider with young drivers is the liability risk to their parents. Because youth are expensive to insure, some people purchase cheaper coverage and put the car in the teen's name, thinking that if the teen is at least eighteen years old and they set things up this way, there will be no exposure to the parent. However, I ran this scenario by some really good attorneys and learned otherwise.

If the parent is still providing support to the teen driver in question, a lawsuit could easily pierce this strategy to go after the parent's assets and wages. Don't take that chance. Your kids are only young for a few years. It's not worth losing everything you've worked for—to say nothing of the fact that you might also have to add 25 percent of your earnings for ten years into the deal—over a few years of temporarily high premiums.

The Other Car

You need to take the driver of the other car into consideration when buying auto coverage. According to a recent *Wall Street Journal* article, 13.8 percent of drivers nationally are uninsured. That number is even greater in California. The Department of Insurance estimated in 2004 that statewide 14.43 percent of all drivers were uninsured, up 5.5 percent from the previous year.

During the fires in 2012, one of my clients in Beverly Hills did a California roll through a stop sign, not realizing that cross traffic didn't have to stop. He collided with a car that was headed into the intersection.

The accident itself wasn't major. Neither vehicle had been moving fast, and it was just a fender bender. However, the passenger in the other car had just had surgery a couple of weeks before the accident. The impact of the collision wouldn't have harmed someone in good health, but it was strong enough that the passenger's surgery needed to be redone.

Because of that, a claim that normally wouldn't have cost more than a few thousand dollars skyrocketed to over $700,000. Fortunately for my client, his umbrella policy stepped in where his auto insurance coverage left off. Otherwise, a lot of very valuable assets would have been at risk. We will discuss umbrella insurance in more detail in chapter 4.

Necessity and Flexibility

Auto insurance is one of those coverage lines where there is no reason to sign up for anything other than complete risk transfer. There is no scenario where it would make more sense to have a hedge, just because it is so easy and it makes so much more sense to get full coverage. When you are covered properly by your auto insurance, your carrier takes complete exposure for anything that might happen on the road, and all you have to do is pay your premium.

As with any form of insurance, there is room for flexibility with auto coverage when it comes to negotiating a price. Auto policies do have deductible-driven features, so you are usually able to strike a balance between those and your monthly payments. For instance, if you wanted more liability coverage but were worried that the payments would break the bank, you could try taking on a higher deductible in order to offset more liability in the event of a claim.

Gap Elimination Checklist

Use the following checklist to begin The Gap Elimination Process™ for auto insurance.

✓ **Additional Equipment:** This generally refers to equipment that is not the vehicle's factory-available equipment. This covers customization of your vehicle done after the factory releases the car to the dealer. If you tend to personalize your car with special wheels and custom interiors, discuss this with your agent. You can cover the cost.

✓ **Auto Death Individual and Specific Disability**: This provides a specific amount of coverage in the event of the death or specified disability of you as the named insured or of your family members due to an accident.

✓ **Bodily Injury:** Bodily injury liability coverage pays in the event that you are legally obligated to pay damages after having caused bodily injury to others in an accident (i.e., a covered loss). Coverage amounts are selectable as a combined single limit (CSL) such as $500,000 or in split limits (such as 250/500/100, etc.). With split limits, the first limit (250) indicates the maximum amount (in thousands of dollars) that can be paid in any one accident to any one person for injury or death. The second limit (500) indicates the maximum amount (in thousands of dollars) that can be paid in any one accident (occurrence) for all persons for injury or death. The third figure (100) is for property damage to houses, cars, light posts, etc. In contrast, a CSL policy offers one lump sum to pay for all of the above. Your bodily injury policy also provides for legal defense costs, subject to provisions in the policy.

✓ **Collision:** This covers physical damage to your insured vehicle (less any deductible selected) when the damage is caused by a collision with another car or object as defined in the policy.

✓ **Comprehensive:** This covers your insured vehicle for physical damage arising from perils other than collision. Examples are theft, fire, earthquake, hitting an animal while driving, and vandalism.

✓ **Broad Form Drive Other Car (BDOC):** This provides coverage if you regularly use a company car. Discuss details with your agent.

✓ **Extended Theft/Stereo/Tapes:** This covers direct and accidental losses to stereo and sound transmission or receiving equipment and accessories that are subject to the provisions of the policy. The comprehensive coverage deductible does not apply to these items. If you have upgraded your sound system after market, you can insure it for theft. Your CD collection can be covered, too.

✓ **Glass Deductible Buyback**: This coverage limits or eliminates the comprehensive coverage deductible for a glass claim. Examples of a glass claim include a chipped, cracked, or pitted windshield. My son was mowing our lawn, and the lawn mower hit a small rock, which flew into the car's side window, shattering the glass. My glass coverage replaced the window with a mobile service at my home. Great coverage at a low cost.

✓ **Medical Coverage:** This is the reasonable cost for necessary medical services, up to the specified amount, due to bodily injury sustained by an insured person or passenger in a covered vehicle accident.

✓ **Property Damage:** Property damage liability coverage will pay for accidental property damage caused by you as an insured driver to someone else's property when you are legally responsible. The policy also provides for legal defense costs, subject to provisions in the policy. Examples of property damage include damage to cars, buildings, street lights, and guard rails. I've seen huge claims to repair guard rails and buildings that would normally be a small claim for the damage done to the car. This is another reason to have umbrella liability that also covers property damage.

✓ **Rental Package–MH/Truck/Van Camper**: This provides coverage as specified in the endorsement when you drive a rented motorhome, truck, van, camper, or other specified rented vehicle.

✓ **Rental Reimbursement Coverage:** This coverage reimburses you for either actual daily rental charges or the purchased limit (whichever is lesser) for a qualified disablement on a covered vehicle. A qualified disablement means that the loss is covered by the comprehensive or collision sections of your policy. Rental reimbursement may be purchased for any vehicle covered by comprehensive and collision coverage. The limit can typically be purchased in varying amounts, such as $50 or $100 a day. If you don't have another car to drive when your car is in the shop due to an accident, be sure to have car rental coverage.

✓ **Rental Trailer/Camper Unit:** This provides coverage as specified in the endorsement for a rented trailer or camper that is towed or attached to your insured vehicle or other specified rented vehicle.

✓ **Residual Debt Coverage:** This covers the additional cost of terminating a finance contract on your insured vehicle in the event of a total loss. For example, if you owe more on your vehicle than the fair market value and the car is totaled, residual debt coverage will cover the amount that you still owe.

✓ **Towing and Road Service:** This covers reasonable and necessary towing and labor costs incurred because of the disablement of your insured car.

✓ **Uninsured Motorist Property Damage:** This pays up to the limit on the policy to repair your car if hit by an uninsured driver.

✓ **Uninsured Motorist Bodily Injury:** This is personal auto insurance that provides coverage for injuries if the insured is involved in an accident with an uninsured, at-fault driver.

✓ **Vehicle Manufacturer Replacement Parts:** Also known as "original equipment manufactured," this provides for replacement of new property or parts made by the original manufacturer, if available. If you want new parts that are made only by the manufacturer of your car, buy this endorsement. Otherwise, your policy will allow rebuilt parts, after-market parts, recycled parts, and parts made by companies other than your carmaker. These after-market parts are not a bad thing and are typically guaranteed by your carrier for as long as you own your car. However, if you're a car buff, you may prefer to pay the extra premium to make sure your car is 100 percent the way you want it.

Never mistake motion for action.

—ERNEST HEMINGWAY

Chapter 4

Umbrella Insurance

The shortest period of time lies between the minute you put some money away for a rainy day and the unexpected arrival of rain.

—JANE BRYANT QUINN

More Than Meets the Eye

A client of mine was driving down Pacific Coast Highway when he dropped a cassette tape on the floor. Without thinking, he reached down to pick it up. His eyes left the road only for a second, but the steering wheel turned sharply to the left. Before he knew what was happening, his car had crossed the double yellow line—straight into the path of an oncoming vehicle.

Considering that it was a head-on collision that took place at fifty miles per hour, everyone involved survived. My client walked away from the scene without serious injuries. The driver he had hit—a young man in his late teens—broke his jaw pretty badly, but survived. When it came to paying for damages, it should have been manageable. A broken jaw is a serious thing, but it doesn't usually work out to a huge amount of money.

However, the teen driver had been slated to star in a Nickelodeon movie. Because of his broken jaw, the filmmakers had to recast his part at the last second. More importantly, it was the kid's big break into the movie industry. The movie was supposed to launch his career as an actor, and his attorney was able to demonstrate that the accident might have destroyed his future. Instantly, a claim that should have been under $100,000 rocketed up to seven figures, plus attorney fees.

My client's auto insurance alone wasn't enough to cover that amount. Moreover, he had a lot of assets—including a business in the community—that could have been in jeopardy. What could have been a life-changing event was averted because of one thing: his umbrella policy. That stepped in where the car insurance left off and paid for the entire claim. Everything was taken care of. Because he was insured correctly, he avoided an "elephant," and everyone was able to move on with their lives.

The Basics of Umbrella Insurance

Umbrella insurance is also known as excess liability coverage. An umbrella policy is designed to pick up where the limit of the underlying policy leaves off.

In the above example, my client had a liability limit on his car of $250,000 for any one person. When that amount of coverage wasn't enough to cover the claim, his umbrella policy kicked in. The same process applies to a liability claim on your home: once the limit of coverage on the policy is exceeded, the umbrella kicks in. Your carrier will require that the policies covered on your umbrella have the required liability limits to qualify. For cars and motorcycles, the limit is typically 250/500/100. For home insurance, the limit is typically $300,000.

Excess liability policies are usually purchased in million-dollar increments—$1 million, $2 million, etc., up to $5 million or more—it depends entirely on how much you feel you need. Individuals with many assets often choose to opt into higher umbrella policies to ensure that they are properly covered. For instance, say you had two people, one whose assets were worth $100,000 and another whose assets were worth $10 million. It wouldn't be unusual for those individuals to have similar auto and home insurance policies. The only difference would be that the person with $10 million in assets would probably have more umbrella coverage.

Another way to look at umbrella policies is to think of them as asset-protection policies. When the liability coverage for your home, cars, boat, motorcycles, rental, or anything else is used up, your umbrella policy kicks in, bringing with it highly trained attorneys and a hefty dose of peace of mind.

The Need for Umbrella Coverage

Not long ago, I did a coverage review with one of my clients in which I increased his umbrella policy to $5 million. Shortly thereafter, he was involved in a very minor car accident. The damage came nowhere near his umbrella limits. Nevertheless, he told me that immediately after impact happened, the first thought in his head was that he was glad that he had increased his umbrella to $5 million. Before making the increase, his assets had been exposed. With the umbrella in place, he felt bulletproof.

Umbrella insurance is more of a necessity than many people

think. Say you are in an accident and get sued. If you are underinsured and have unprotected assets, the plaintiff has the option of bypassing your insurance policy and just going after you personally, thereby rendering your insurance inadequate. In a situation like that, your policy would be part of the settlement and you—or more accurately, your assets and future income—would pay the rest.

Depending on your carrier, you may be able to get coverage on your umbrella policy that goes beyond just having more liability. For example, some carriers will provide coverage for employment practices liability, include coverage if you are on the board of a nonprofit organization, and offer excess liability coverage when driving abroad.

When you consider the ratio of the monthly premium versus the thousands of dollars of coverage you receive for it, umbrella liability policy is one of the least expensive types of insurance policies you can buy. Considering that umbrella is the only coverage that truly provides asset protection, including one of these policies in your insurance portfolio and keeping it up to date is an absolute must.

Uninsured motorist is an endorsement that is often overlooked on an umbrella. Some carriers don't even offer it. It provides additional coverage if the uninsured motorist limit on the car policy is not enough. For example, say you have $250,000 of uninsured motorist on your car and $1 million of uninsured motorist on your umbrella. You now have $1.25 million of coverage for yourself and $1.5 million for other passengers in your car (combined, not each). It acts as if the person who hit you had an insurance policy for $1.5 million.

An agent friend told me a story about his client who was turning on Ventura Boulevard in California's San Fernando Valley while a police chase was going on. The fleeing vehicle was on the wrong side of the road and slammed into the client's car at high speed. There were three people in the client's car—husband, wife, and child. All three were injured. The wife had three surgeries and still can't walk. The husband wasn't hurt nearly as badly and had to work twice as much to make up for the loss of his wife's income. They had $250,000 of uninsured motorist on their auto policy, but they did not have uninsured motorist on their umbrella. It would have made a world of difference if they had. In hindsight, spending $200 extra for the endorsements would have made a huge difference in helping them through this unfortunate experience.

Gap Elimination Checklist

Use the following checklist to begin The Gap Elimination Process™ for umbrella insurance.

- ✓ **Additional Motorized Vehicles**: Make sure that each car you have is listed on your umbrella policy.

- ✓ **Additional Owner Occupied Residences**: Additional residences, whether secondary or seasonal, can be covered by your umbrella insurance. Make sure all homes you own, including vacant land, are listed.

- ✓ **Child Care Liability**: Child care liability is excluded on personal umbrella policies. However, if child care liability coverage is furnished on the underlying personal liability policy, this coverage may be added to the personal umbrella. Ask your agent about the possibility of setting this up.

- ✓ **Director and Officers of Nonprofits**: If you sit on the board of a nonprofit, you may be able to add coverage to your umbrella.

✓ **Excluding Uninsured/Underinsured Motorist Coverage**: This endorsement deletes uninsured/underinsured motorist coverage from the umbrella policy. The only reason to do this is to save on premiums.

✓ **Incidental Business Pursuits**: An incidental business may be covered for an additional premium. The business must be covered on an underlying liability policy for this additional coverage to become available.

✓ **Loss Assessment Endorsement**: Loss assessment applies when you live in a home that has an association with common areas. If a claim in a common area would have been covered if it was within your home, then it is most likely covered under your assessment coverage, unless there are specific exclusions. Common exclusions are earthquake and flood. In order for loss assessment coverage to apply, you'll need to have the required limit on your home policy, which is typically $50,000, and have loss assessment endorsed to your umbrella. With this endorsement, if you are assessed for property damage or for a liability claim that applies to your policy, you'll be covered. This is a much-overlooked endorsement. If you are in a homeowners association, you will need this whether it's a condo or townhome or single-family residence. Otherwise, if there is an assessment for a liability or other specific type of property coverage on a common area, you will have to pay out of pocket.

✓ **Rental Dwellings**: A rental unit is defined as one living quarter, either stand-alone or within a larger space. There may be multiple units per dwelling. Make sure each rental you own is shown on your umbrella policy.

✓ **Uninsured/Underinsured Motorist Coverage (UM/UIM):** If UM/UIM coverage is desired, it must be written and rated on all the scheduled underlying auto exposures, including automobiles, trucks, motor homes, motorcycles, licensed recreational vehicles, broad form use of another car, and licensed golf carts. In order to have uninsured motorist apply to your umbrella, you'll need to have the required limit for uninsured motorist on your car or motorcycle, which typically is $250,000. The umbrella will also need to be endorsed for uninsured motorist and an additional premium will apply. Most carriers that allow an uninsured motorist endorsement to their umbrella will limit the amount to $1 million. By having uninsured motorist on your umbrella, your policy will provide the limits you select for yourself and your family. It acts as if the person who hit you had the limits.

✓ **Unlicensed Recreational Vehicles:** This is coverage for vehicles designed primarily for off-road recreational use.

✓ **Watercraft:** This coverage includes jet skis and jet sleds, sailboats, inboards, inboard/outboards, outboards, and power boats.

⟳

Chapter 5

Life Insurance

In all things that you do, consider the end.

—SOLON

The Helicopter Accident

Years ago, a young couple came into my office with their two-year-old daughter. They wanted to sign up for home insurance, car insurance, and umbrella insurance; they needed everything. I walked them through the process, and everything went smoothly until we hit the life insurance policy.

Suddenly, the husband—who had been on board with everything else—started resisting. He was young and healthy, he said. He didn't need life insurance.

Meanwhile, despite having been in the business for only a few years, I had seen the consequences of skipping out on life insurance. I was a believer. I was passionate about life insurance. So I sat with them and made the argument in favor of a life insurance policy, and fortunately he finally came around. The coverage they settled on was worth $1 million—not as much as they needed, but it was better than nothing. Everyone left the office satisfied.

About six months later, I got a phone call from my client's brother. At first, I assumed that he was a referral. Then he told me the real reason for calling. "My brother was a commercial film producer," he said. "He was filming a commercial up in Canada, and the helicopter he was in exploded during takeoff. Nobody survived."

I was speechless. All I could think about was that day they had come to see me six months before, when I had made the extra effort to explain why life insurance was so important.

A week later, when his widow came to meet me, I handed her a check for $1 million. Because of that money, she was able to stay in her house, and her daughter was able to grow up and graduate from high school in our community. Without the life insurance policy, their lives would have been dramatically different—another "elephant" avoided.

The Basics of Life Insurance

Everyone is quick to acknowledge the importance of homeowners, auto, or umbrella insurance, but life insurance isn't something that people tend to automatically buy. However, life insurance isn't dispensable. It's not something that should be an afterthought or a footnote when putting together your insurance portfolio. As terrible as losing a house may be, it is worth a fixed amount. With life insurance, you are talking about losing the source that generated the money to buy that house in the first place, and the financial impact of that is enormous.

It isn't just people with dangerous jobs who need to seriously look into buying life insurance. The unexpected happens to people every day, and none of them are any more prepared for it than my client was when he got into the helicopter that morning.

Another man I knew was perfectly healthy, but took out a life insurance policy for just under $1 million anyway. Two years later, he started getting severe headaches. It turned out that he had developed an inoperable brain tumor. A couple of months later, he was gone, just like that. The life insurance claim paid to his family upon his death helped his kids finish college. When his wife sold the house, she did it because she wanted to, not because she had to.

Life insurance is first and foremost a hedge. It is designed to mitigate all or part of a risk. Once you own your policy, you are guaranteed a certain amount of money should something happen to you during a fixed and agreed-upon period of time. You choose the period. That period can be anywhere from one year to well over age one hundred.

For example, when a couple buys a $1 million home, they know they will pay the mortgage for several years. They want to make certain that if something happens to one of them as a wage earner before the mortgage is paid, the remainder of what is owed will be taken care of. That can be done with a term policy. The couple would just calculate how many years they expect to hold the mortgage, and purchase a life insurance policy that covers the fixed period of time.

Term policies are a great fit for certain needs, but they aren't necessarily a one-size-fits-all plan for life insurance. For instance, if your primary goal is to pass your assets on to your children, a term policy is not going to be the best choice for you, because it's possible that you will outlive the term period.

In fact, carriers are able to price term policies at such reasonable rates because they are reasonably sure that you won't end up using the coverage. Less than 2 percent of term policies ever end up in a claim. The younger and further away from life expectancy you are, the cheaper term life insurance is because your chance of dying is so low. As you grow older, the price for life insurance increases, and when you start approaching life expectancy the cost becomes astronomical. For that reason, finding someone at life expectancy who has a term policy is extremely rare. With that said, I have paid out many millions of dollars to beneficiaries of term insurance.

Not all forms of life insurance are term policies. Permanent policies are also available. These policies can be designed to last through life expectancy. A few examples of permanent life insurance policies include Universal Life, Whole Life, Variable Life, and Guaranteed Universal Life. The variations of these permanent policies are almost endless. Below is a brief overview of some of the more common forms to show you how they work.

Universal Life

Universal Life insurance is designed to last for as long as you choose, provided the interest rate that was assumed when you took out the policy remains accurate.

For every dollar you put into a Universal Life policy, part of it pays for the mortality expense (the life insurance part), another part pays for the policy fees, and the rest goes into the cash accumulation side of the policy. The amount in the cash accumulation side of the policy will get credited and grow by the interest rate the carrier sets. When interest rates are high, the policy will grow by a higher rate of interest; when rates are low, the growth will be lower.

The problem with these policies arises when interest rates are low and not enough premiums have been paid to adequately pay for the mortality and policy fees. As you grow older, the mortality fees increase. If your cash accumulation side of the policy doesn't grow fast enough, the balance in that accumulation account can actually start to decrease to the point that over time there won't be enough to pay for the mortality expense, and the policy will lapse if premiums are not increased.

In order to make sure this doesn't happen, use an estimated rate of interest that is reasonable (low) when looking at a policy illustration. The policy illustration is prepared when initially designing the policy. It shows how the policy will perform over time, provided the premium shown is paid and the rate of interest shown is achieved on average over the years.

These types of policies created problems for people, who bought them assuming a rate of interest at 7, 8, 9, or 10 percent on average, and ended up getting an average of 3–4 percent per year.

A Universal policy is an excellent policy choice to fund a longer-term need. It won't expire like a term policy, but watch out for the illustrated rate of interest and make sure you pay enough to pay for the long term.

Whole Life

Whole Life insurance provides coverage during your entire lifetime at a fixed premium. Whole Life insurance is the most basic type of permanent coverage. The insurance company makes all the decisions on the cash accumulation side of the policy. A fixed death benefit is paid, along with what is accumulated on the cash side.

Variable Universal Life

A Variable Universal Life policy is like a Universal Life policy, except instead of the cash accumulation side getting credited at a rate of interest set by the carrier, the policy provides sub accounts through which you can direct the accumulation side of the policy. You'll have many allocation choices for your funds, including mutual funds, stock indexes, and bond funds. By leveraging this extra control over your investments, you gain the potential to make the accumulation side of your policy perform better than it would in a traditional interest-rate policy.

Neither Universal Life nor Variable Universal Life policies, however, come with a guarantee. If interest rates or the market go down, that may directly affect your expectation of the accumulation side of your policy in a negative way.

Guaranteed Universal Life

Because of the lack of guarantee with both Universal Life and Variable Universal Life policies, and a high demand for a guarantee by many consumers, the industry designed a Guaranteed Universal Life policy. With this type of life insurance policy, you choose how long you want your coverage to be guaranteed for. You can set the age to whatever makes you comfortable. The premium for a Guaranteed Universal Life policy is similar to that of a traditional Universal Life policy. However, in exchange for the guarantee, you give up the potential for robust growth of the cash accumulation side. Guaranteed Universal Life policies are an excellent choice for those who want the certainty of a death benefit at a particular age and are not concerned about accessing the accumulation side of their policy at a later date.

Converting Term Life Insurance

Term insurance is written for a period of time (e.g., five, ten, twenty, or thirty years). Check if your term policy is convertible to a permanent policy without having to underwrite it. If so, all you'll have to do is sign the new permanent policy. You won't need to redo the medical exam. When you do convert the term policy to a permanent one, your rate will be based on the age of when you convert. Some policies will only let you convert without underwriting during part of the time period you've selected. As an example, a twenty-year term policy may only allow for a conversion without underwriting during the first ten years that you have it.

The Uses of Life Insurance

Many people assume that there is only one use for life insurance: someone passes away unexpectedly, and the carrier pays the agreed amount to the survivors.

Nothing could be further from the truth. There are hundreds of uses for life insurance. It can help with funding future events and trusts to filling income replacement when the need arises. Here are some of the many possibilities of leveraging life insurance.

Estate Tax Funding

Under the current tax code, the federal estate tax will exempt approximately the first $5 million of inheritance. Even if you are not subject to the estate tax, having a guaranteed pot of money available to you that can be accessed quickly can only work to your advantage. In some cases, it may enable you to hold on to certain assets until it is an ideal time to sell them, rather than being forced to put them on the market wholesale before their time. If life insurance is purchased early enough, this amounts to literally buying dollars with pennies. By going the extra mile and planning for the future with a simple Irrevocable Life Insured Trust (ILIT), the life insurance benefit you leave for your children can be 100 percent tax free.

Gifting

In advanced cases, gifting can play a huge role in leveraging wealth. Let's say a couple with a decent net worth decide to pass on a specific amount of that money to their kids, grandkids, charity, or whatever else. That couple probably have investments, but they may not know for certain whether those investments will grow the way they would ideally like them to, in which case they may not be confident of having the amount of money that they want to pass on to their heirs. With life insurance, you can guarantee that an exact amount of money will be there for your beneficiaries, as long as the premiums have been paid.

You can take this process a step further by paying those life in-surance premiums via gifting. Gifting is when you give money to the beneficiary of the life policy to pay the premium. The gift is tax free to the beneficiary provided it does not exceed the annual maximum, which is $13,000 as of 2013. You may gift to each child and grand-child that maximum amount, as can your spouse.

When you go this route, the amount used to pay the premium is taken out of the estate, meaning that those funds are no longer a part of the estate itself and can therefore be leveraged by many multiples. As long as the policy in question is held in a properly structured ILIT (Irrevocable Life Insured Trust), your beneficiaries will pay zero taxes when they receive the money. Using this strategy, your gifting goals can be 100 percent guaranteed and tax free. Moreover, you have the security and confidence you need to invest the remaining assets of the estate more aggressively than you would have if the amount to your beneficiaries were not guaranteed.

Another example of a scenario where life insurance can offer unexpected benefits comes in the form of special needs cases. The cost of providing for someone's special needs—be it a parent, a spouse, or a child—can be crippling over a long period of time. Life insurance owned by a special needs trust can guarantee continuity of care, giving you the assurance that your loved one will be taken care of. Any type of life insurance can fund this, but a permanent policy is strongly recommended since the policy will not expire, as is the case with a term policy.

Taking Care of Business Partners

Another lesser-known use of life insurance is available to those who own businesses. In business, it's typical to have a partner, and for each partner to have a spouse. If one business partner dies, the spouse of the deceased usually becomes the new business partner—even if he or she doesn't have the experience to do the job or the personal chemistry to work with the remaining partner.

In situations like these, if the surviving partner doesn't have enough funds to buy out the spouse of the deceased one, a forced sale of the business frequently takes place. To solve this problem, you can set up a life insurance policy in conjunction with a buy/sell agreement that determines the value of the business. This provides the necessary funds to pay the surviving spouse in full for his or her share of the business, leaving the remaining partner with 100 percent ownership.

Using Life Insurance Funds

The amount of life insurance purchased when a policy is bought may sound like a lot of money at the time. But I have never heard a beneficiary receiving the check say, "Oh, this is an amazing amount of money. I have no idea what I'm going to do with it." On the contrary, the more common response is, "I don't know how I'm going to make it." You don't want to use the life insurance money itself to pay for your day-to-day living costs. You want to use that initial lump sum to generate income.

For instance, say you receive $1 million, and you are fortunate enough to get a 5 percent return on that money. In that case, what you are really earning is $50,000 a year, and that is before taxes. After that, your income may be closer to $40,000 a year. If you need more than that and have to start dipping into the capital of the policy itself, $1 million is not that much. That should be your thought process when you consider life insurance coverage.

In my experience, when a loved one is lost, a family gets deluged with bills and condolences. I've had the honor to bring a check with my condolences and share the story of when the policy was taken out and the love that was there; the story of how their loved one cared for them and trusted me to bring this check if the unspeakable occurred. It is always a moving experience, and I've always felt privileged to be a part of it.

When it comes to life insurance, the question each of us needs to ask ourselves is what legacy we want to leave. That might mean taking care of a spouse, a child, or a business partner. It might mean leaving grants, scholarships, or endowments for future generations.

Whatever the case, your individual ideal legacy can be provided for with a little imagination and some planning and trust work.

Another strategy can be used for a parent or grandparent to fund a legacy using life insurance that is guaranteed. Once set up, the legacy is assured to take place and is funded. It would be incredibly satisfying to have set something up that funds the legacy that you designed.

Using this strategy may also allow you to invest your remaining assets for a potentially greater return, since you no longer have to be concerned about shielding the portion of your assets allocated to your legacy from risk in the market.

One of the best lines I've heard in this business is "Life Insurance is for the living." Each dollar that the living receive after you pass away is a result of your thoughtfulness and a memory of the love you shared.

Gap Elimination Checklist

Before you get started, review your original intent in buying a life insurance policy. Was it to pay off debt, fund education, provide income, or something else? Whatever it was, things have a way of changing.

Make sure the coverage amount is right for your current and anticipated needs. If you already have a policy in place, now is the time to amend and adjust.

Use the following checklist to begin The Gap Elimination Process™ for life insurance.

✓ **Assumption Policy** (AP): These policies show an assumed performance based on certain premiums being paid, assuming a certain rate of interest. An illustration is provided when you purchase it that shows the expected performance. If you have had an assumption policy such as Universal Life or Variable Life for a while, ask your carrier for an "in-force" illustration. The carrier will send you an illustration that shows how your policy is currently doing and is anticipated to do based on today's rates. Ordering the in-force illustration every few years will allow you to avoid surprises in the future.

✓ **Beneficiary Designation:** If your beneficiary is your spouse, you typically won't have a taxable event upon death. However, if your beneficiary is anyone else, the taxes on the death benefit can be substantial. Talk to your insurance broker about strategies to eliminate the taxes. The easiest way is to have the beneficiary own the policy and pay the premium. Gifting the premium to the beneficiary may be possible, as well.

✓ **Contingent Beneficiary:** A contingent beneficiary is someone who will receive life insurance proceeds if the primary beneficiary is not alive when the insured is deceased. Minors are not a good choice to use as a contingent beneficiary, as the carrier cannot send a check to a minor. Make sure your will states what should happen to your minor children in the event of the death of both spouses, and coordinate this directive with the contingent beneficiary designation if minors are involved.

✓ **Guaranteed Policy** (GP): These policies are written up to a specific age—95, 100, 105, etc. They were designed to fix the issue AP (Assumption Policy) policies had when they didn't perform as expected following the financial crisis. Once you know how much premium you need to pay up to the guaranteed age limit, be careful to never pay more or less than that, because that could void the guarantee. A GP is designed to have a protected death benefit up to the stated age. Unlike with an AP, there is very little cash accumulation. An AP policy is purchased strictly for the guarantee of the death benefit. GPs are the policy of choice for estate planning, since the premium and the death benefit are both guaranteed and cash-value accumulation is not a concern.

✓ **Premium Payment Methods:** Most carriers charge more if you want to pay your premiums monthly. Some charge significantly more for the monthly payment option. If you pay monthly premiums, check the annual cost of paying monthly versus the annual cost of paying in one lump sum.

◯✕✕✕✕◯

Chapter 6

Long-Term Care

Do not regret growing older.
It is a privilege denied to many.

—AUTHOR UNKNOWN

Rosa's Story

Most people associate insurance for long-term care (LTC) with nursing homes, and it does include that coverage. However, LTC insurance actually has a wider scope than it usually gets credit for.

One example of the flexibility of long-term care insurance is illustrated by the story of a client named Rosa. She could brighten a room just by walking into it. Rosa had been a stage actress when she was young, and she loved to talk. Every time she saw you, she would ask all about your life: How is your spouse? How is your dog? Did you get that promotion? You knew that she truly cared about the answers.

Rosa had all her policies with us, so I knew her well. She was single, and her kids did not live in the area, so while we were reviewing her coverage one year, we decided that it would be a good idea for her to sign up for a long-term care policy. Rosa was in her sixties at the time, and not nearly ready for a nursing home. But given her situation and the fact that it was less expensive to sign up early, she felt it was the right thing to do.

As it turned out, about six months after having that policy in force, Rosa was in a terrible car accident. She survived, but for about four months she was not able to do anything. She spent that time at home convalescing, but the silver lining was that her long-term care policy covered those costs. Because of her injuries, Rosa could not perform basic activities such as feeding, bathing, and dressing herself—the same kinds of things that trigger coverage in a LTC policy. So her policy took effect, enabling her to have someone else help with those basic activities until she made a full recovery.

Rosa kept the same LTC policy, and a few years later it came to the aid of her and her family a second time. By now, Rosa, who was in her seventies, was starting to experience some serious health issues. A home health-care provider looked after her in her house for a couple of years, until her condition worsened and she needed to be transferred to a nursing care facility in Santa Monica, California. The home was a beautiful place.

I lived in the same neighborhood, so I often stopped in to visit her with my German shepherd, Jasso, whom Rosa was always thrilled to see. Rosa spent almost two years in that nursing facility before she passed away.

Two or three months later, Rosa's son and daughter turned up at my office, to my surprise. They said they wanted me to hear in person that the long-term care policy I had arranged for their mother was the reason they had gotten an inheritance from her. It had made a huge impact on their lives.

"Thank you so much for bringing it up and making the effort to put it in place," they said. "Thank you."

It was a new perspective for me, and I was genuinely moved.

The Basics of Long-Term Care

Long-term care (LTC) can help you avoid the "elephant" of health-care costs when you are debilitated. LTC is a person's necessity or requirement to have assistance. Most people will need long-term care at some point in their lives. LTC policies are triggered when someone is unable to perform two out of the six listed Activities of Daily Living (ADLs): bathing, continence, dressing, eating, toileting, and transferring. Cognitive impairment, such as Alzheimer's disease, provides automatic coverage. Once a doctor has verified that a person can't handle a minimum of two of the activities without aid, the LTC policy takes effect.

Having LTC may let you avail of the care you need sooner. LTC gives you the resources to afford quality care and the freedom to choose how the care is performed, without draining your own resources in the process. Without LTC, many individuals wouldn't have the funds to choose from all the options that would otherwise be available to them.

For example, most people who need assistance with day-to-day living prefer to stay in their own homes as long as possible. The cost of trained, live-in health-care professionals is covered by LTC. Then, if the person needs more advanced care, LTC pays for a nursing home.

LTC coverage has become increasingly expensive. In 2013, the cost of long-term care was close to $300 a day, which adds up to $9,000 a month or $100,000 a year. Although some individuals only need long-term care for a couple of years, others rely on it for much longer. My own grandmother moved into a long-term care facility in Belleview, Washington, when she was in her mid-seventies and stayed there until she was 101 years old. Every case is different, and it's important to assess the situation clearly before signing up for an LTC policy.

How to Pay for Long-Term Care

One aspect of long-term care coverage that many people are unaware of is that LTC policies can be written for different periods of time. That might be for two years, five years, ten years, or for life. Regardless, the policy can be designed to fit the needs and budget of the person buying it. If lifetime LTC is unaffordable, a person still has the option of hedging by purchasing coverage for a few years. This could at least extend the period of time before the individual is forced to use all assets, if not eliminate the need to do that altogether.

There are five standard ways to pay for long-term care.

Option 1: Use cash. Some people have the resources to set money aside for LTC on their own. They plan accordingly, and when the time comes, they cover the cost of LTC themselves out of pocket.

Option 2: Buy a traditional LTC policy. These have been around for a long time. They pay for home health care and a nursing home. Depending on how you want to address your potential long-term care need, you can buy as much or as little LTC coverage as you need.

One issue with a traditional policy is that there is no guarantee that premiums will remain the same. Most carriers say they don't intend to increase rates, but lately a few have done so. If the claims experience of a carrier is poor, you may experience a rate increase.

Option 3: Get a linked benefit annuity. An annuity is a tax-deferred savings vehicle. In a linked benefit annuity, you buy the annuity and get a long-term care endorsement on it. For example, say you decide to put $100,000 in an annuity. That money will earn a certain amount of tax-deferred interest on an annual basis. In addition, you have a long-term-care benefit rider working on this. Most insurance carriers will give you a multiple of the face amount of the annuity you've created in the event that you need to withdraw funds for the purposes of long-term care.

Let's say your benefit rider gave you a multiple of two on your annuity. You put $100,000 into the annuity and make $10,000 in interest before you need to start withdrawing the money for long-term care. Because of the multiple of two on your policy, you can withdraw double the $110,000 in your annuity—or $220,000—to cover the care you need. Moreover, if you never need to use that money for long-term care, it will continue to grow tax-deferred on an annual basis, and you won't lose a dime. However, this type of annuity is not available in all states. Your agent can tell you whether it is available where you live.

Option 4: Take out a life insurance policy with a long-term care rider. In this option, you are basically purchasing a pool of money. Let's say you wanted to buy $500,000 that could be used for long-term care. At $100,000 a year, that money would cover the cost of your care for about five years. That money will be available when you need to pay for long-term care. However, if you never use it or only use some of it, the remaining balance goes to your beneficiaries. With this option, you are repositioning an asset. It dramatically leverages your premium. Another advantage of the long-term care rider on a life policy is that most carriers offer a guaranteed premium till life expectancy. You may have less of a chance of experiencing a rate increase.

Option 5: This is used as a last resort. If you become destitute with assets of less than $2,000 and can't afford to buy LTC coverage, you can apply for Medicaid, and the state government may cover the cost of your care for you. Medicaid will then take whatever income you have, and leave you with $35 a month for personal items.

Some people think that their Medicare policy will provide some long-term care. It's a false sense of security. For Medicare to pay for long-term care, you first have to be hospitalized for at least three nights and then transferred to an approved nursing home within thirty days of release. Even then, only twenty days of LTC are paid at 100 percent. After that up to a hundred days, you'll have a daily co-payment of $137.50 per day, and that's if you even qualify.

None of these five options is a one-size-fits-all solution. What works well for someone else may not be the best option for you. Everyone should take the time to review the options carefully and decide on a long-term-care policy that makes sense for his or her situation.

When to Buy Long-Term Care Insurance

As you should with any insurance product, examine carefully in advance which LTC option will best fit your needs. Most people don't want to start thinking seriously about long-term care until they are close to actually needing it, at which point coverage becomes incredibly expensive. Although the cost difference varies depending on which carrier you choose, most of them can provide an illustration called the Cost of Waiting, which shows how much extra you'll have to pay for every year you wait, provided that you can qualify for the coverage. If you apply when you are younger and healthier, you will get a much better deal.

In my experience, people begin to think seriously about long-term care coverage in their mid-fifties because many of them see their parents starting to need long-term care. The natural process then is to start thinking about preparing for their own futures. Those who sign up for LTC coverage in their mid-fifties usually pay dramatically less than those who purchase it in their mid-sixties. Over that ten-year difference, the cost of most LTC policies can double.

Gap Elimination Checklist

Use the following checklist to walk yourself through The Gap Elimination Process™ for long-term care.

✓ **Maximum Daily Benefit:** This is the maximum amount that your carrier will reimburse you for each day of qualified care you receive.

✓ **Benefit Period**: This is the number of days for which you wish to receive benefits. The benefit period is selected at the time of application.

✓ **Maximum Lifetime Benefit Amount**: This is the total amount of benefits reimbursable under the policy for your long-term care and services. The maximum lifetime benefit amount is determined by multiplying your selected maximum daily benefit amount by the number of days in your selected benefit period.

✓ **Maximum Monthly Benefit**: This represents the dollar benefit amount available to you on a monthly basis for your long-term care needs. The original dollar amount is calculated as a percentage of the lifetime benefit amount.

✓ **Maximum Residential Care Facility Benefit Amount and Maximum Home-Care and Community-Based Services Benefit Amount**: If you are eligible, this is the maximum amount reimbursable for the qualified expenses that you incur for LTC services provided by a residential care facility, a home health-care agency, an independent care provider, or an adult day care facility. This includes home health care, adult day care, personal care, or homemaker services, such as helping you with the activities of daily living, housekeeping, preparing meals, and physical therapy.

✓ **Daily Benefit Increase Rider**: This increases your current maximum daily benefit annually by 5 percent at either a compound or a simple rate, with no maximum daily benefit ceiling. The increase occurs each year during policy renewal and is designed to keep up with inflation.

✓ **Simple Benefit Increase Rider/Simple Inflation Rider**: Under this rider, the benefit increases by a fixed amount per year, not on a compounded basis.

✓ **Automatic Compound Benefit Increase Options**: If this rider is chosen, the original maximum monthly benefit of the policy automatically increases by the percentage selected, such as 3 percent or 5 percent, each year on a compounded basis. The increase will take effect on each anniversary of the policy-effective date, even while benefits are being received.

✓ **Bed Reservation**: If you are absent for any reason except discharge during confinement in a nursing home or residential care, the policy will provide up to thirty days per calendar year of benefits for the actual charges incurred to reserve your room, up to the maximum nursing home or residential care facility benefit stated on your policy. An example would be if you left the facility for a few days to go to your grandchild's wedding.

✓ **Elimination Period**: This is the number of days you are responsible for paying the cost of covered long-term care services before your policy begins to pay benefits. You actually need to pay for care during this period to qualify.

✓ **Free Look Period:** You have thirty days to review your policy after purchasing it. If you decide it's not for you, you can simply return the policy and get a refund of all the premiums.

✓ **Benefit Triggers**: This refers to the inability of a person to perform a minimum of two of the six ADLs: bathing, continence, dressing, eating, toileting, and transferring. Cognitive impairment such as Alzheimer's disease triggers automatic coverage.

✓ **Caregiver Training Benefit**: This covers the cost of training for an informal caregiver or an immediate family member to perform maintenance and personal care services in the home. The full cost or part of it may be covered, based on the policy.

✓ **Couples Discount:** Couples may be eligible for a discount of up to 30 percent on LTC policies, as compared to standard individual rates.

✓ **Family Discount:** When you and two other family members own separate individual LTC policies, each will receive a 5 percent discount. Please check policy details to determine what type of family discount is available for particular kinds of LTC. Some LTC products may only allow immediate family members, while others may extend to in-laws, grandparents, cousins, etc.

✓ **Global/International Coverage Benefit**: This allows you to be anywhere in the world and still have some coverage under your LTC insurance policy, such as 50 percent nursing facility, 25 percent home care for 365 days, or a 48-month limit. Please review the benefit limits on any LTC product before purchasing it. The coverage varies depending on the product and carrier.

✓ **Graded Return of Premium upon Death Rider**: This rider adds a benefit to your policy to refund a percentage of premiums paid, less the amount of any benefits reimbursed or reimbursable upon your death, if your death occurs before your seventy-fifth birthday.

✓ **Guaranteed Future Purchase Offer Rider**: Under this rider, an insurer offers to increase the policyholder's current lifetime benefit amount and the maximum monthly benefit by a certain percentage every two or three years without having to meet underwriting requirements anew. The negative is that the cost of each new offer will be based on the latest age of the covered individual. Many insurers will stop making such offers if they are rejected two or more times. The typical cost of this inflation rider is 2 percent of the premium. Experts think this is a good option for individuals who are in their seventies.

✓ **Home Modification and Supplemental Products Benefit**: This benefit offers services or products that are required by a chronically ill person in order to live at home, including home modifications, emergency response systems, and durable medical equipment.

✓ **Hospice Services**: If you are eligible, the policy will provide daily benefits for each day you receive services from a hospice program. The benefits are paid on the actual charges incurred up to an individual's maximum nursing home benefit.

✓ **Shortened Benefit Non-Forfeiture Option Rider**: If a policy is in force for at least three full years and then terminated due to non-payment of premiums, this optional rider allows for a reduced amount of coverage. For example, if you originally bought a $300-a-day policy and stopped paying for it after five years, the carrier will determine how much daily benefit you'll have going forward without having to pay additional premiums.

✓ **Pool of Money**: Your policy's maximum is the total amount available to cover the cost of your long-term care services.

✓ **Preferred Health Discount**: Individuals who have taken care of their health may be rewarded with a discount of up to 10 percent off standard premium rates.

✓ **Respite Care**: These services provide short-term care for you while your informal unpaid caregiver in the home takes a brief rest.

✓ **Restoration of Benefits**: If you received benefits and recuperated with the result that you no longer received qualified LTC services for a period of 180 consecutive days, all benefits that were paid, except for global coverage benefits, will be restored to the remaining policy maximum amount.

✓ **Return of Premium upon Death Rider**: While the policy is in force, and if your death occurs before the first policy anniversary date following your eightieth birthday, the insurer will pay a return on your premium benefits.

✓ **Waiver of Premium**: Premiums are waived beginning on the first day that the policyholder starts receiving benefits. The waiver continues throughout the benefit period. Premium payments resume after thirty days of not receiving benefits.

✓ **Joint Waiver of Premium Rider**: This rider ensures that when one member of a couple becomes eligible for the Waiver of Premium benefit, both members have their premiums waived.

✓ **Survivor Benefit Rider:** This rider adds a benefit that waives premiums for your policy in the event that your spouse or domestic partner dies, provided that both of the insured have purchased the rider and that both policies have been in effect for at least ten years.

✓ **Shared Care Rider:** This rider gives couples the ability to share their lifetime benefit amounts with one another.

✓ **Shared Extended Benefit Rider:** This option allows couples to share an additional extended pool of benefits in the event that one or both exhaust their benefits.

☙

*Youth would be an ideal state if it came
a little later in life.*

—HERBERT HENRY ASQUITH

Chapter 7

Disability

The greatest wealth is health.

—VIRGIL

Facing Down Thyroid Cancer

Recently, I met a friend I had not seen in several months. As soon as I saw him, I knew something was wrong. He looked thin and pale—not like his usual healthy self at all.

"What happened?" I asked.

"Thyroid cancer," he replied.

My friend had been undergoing treatments, which had been taking their toll on him. He said he didn't know if he would be cured. The disease was advanced enough, and the future was uncertain. He might recover, or he might not live at all. Or he might survive, but be unable to work for the rest of his life.

Still, he told me, no matter what happened, he was ready for it. If he died, his kids would be able to finish their college education, and his wife would be taken care of for the rest of her life. If he lived but was unable to go back to work, that was taken care of, too. He had enough disability insurance so that he could continue to bring in an income, and his standard of living wouldn't be dramatically impacted.

That made a powerful impression on me. Here was a man who, because he had the right philosophy about insurance, was able to face down a life-changing situation. He didn't have to think, "What am I going to do to support myself if I can't work?" or "What will my family do if I die?" That was already taken care of. The only stress or pressure that he had to deal with was getting well.

My friend did beat his thyroid cancer. And his disability insurance covered him through his recovery. But throughout the experience, he had the comfort of knowing that no matter what happened, he did not have to face the "elephant" of disability alone.

The Basics of Disability Insurance

Disability insurance covers you when you need to replace your income. As with life insurance, most people don't consider disability insurance essential until it's too late. In reality, the biggest monetary loss that an individual can possibly face is an inability to earn an income.

Let's say you're a doctor making $250,000 a year. However, if someone hits you on the road and you need to spend five or six months in physical therapy learning how to walk again, that's going to stop you from doing your job and making money. Suddenly, your whole lifestyle is in jeopardy.

The idea behind disability insurance is that you need to insure the goose that lays the golden egg. You need to insure your ability to sustain yourself and your family in case you can't work and support them. Those who have signed up for life insurance can rest easy that funds will come in for the people they leave behind. Everyone tends to think about this in terms of life and death, but few people stop to consider the middle ground: you may not die, but you may not be able to do to the work you used to do if you live, either.

Ideally, you want to risk-transfer your income to an insurance company for a fairly reasonable premium. As with any kind of insurance coverage, everything relates to risk and rewards. How much of your lifetime earnings' loss can you transfer to a company, and what will it cost? Generally, the cost involved is a small percentage of a person's income. The Gap Elimination Checklist for this chapter will help identify the best disability coverage for you.

What Disability Insurance Covers

When people think about disability insurance, they may imagine it is for someone in a warehouse who gets run over by a lift truck. But disability insurance may cover more than you think. Disability can include all kinds of things. Depending on your occupation, your disability policy could cover an inability to work due to emotional stress, complications with a pregnancy, and other specific conditions that interfere with your ability to do your job.

For instance, I have a veterinarian friend who has a clinic and does surgery on animals. If something happened to prevent him from being able to perform surgery, he could earn an income through his clinic practice, but his disability policy would still compensate him because technically he is losing income due to his inability to operate on animals. There is a lot more flexibility in disability insurance than many people tend to assume.

Who Should Buy Disability Insurance

Anyone with a demonstrably repeatable income is a good candidate for disability insurance.

For example, my veterinarian friend might make $100,000 a year. His business has been around for several years, and that income is stable. He could submit his income history to an underwriter to prove that he does make $100,000 steadily every year, and the underwriter would look at that and say, "Great, I can set you up with a disability policy for a minimal premium."

On the other hand, another client of mine is an artist with a wildly fluctuating income. That made it challenging to find disability insurance for her. Most carriers didn't want to underwrite her case, and those that did were unwilling to provide all of the endorsements that I like to see on a disability policy, such as paying for benefits up to the age of sixty-five and paying a high percentage of her earnings.

Generally speaking, then, anybody who has an income that they can demonstrate is repeatable should consider having disability insurance. These would typically include white-collar professionals such as doctors, lawyers, administrators, and other high-income earners who would be at a distinct disadvantage if they were to be impacted by a disability that created a significant drop in their usual income.

For these people, risk-transferring their income to an insurance company can usually be done for a minimal amount of money. Once purchased, a disability policy will often pay the lost income all the way to the individual's retirement age—typically sixty-five or seventy years old. This takes place regardless of the person's age at the time of the disablement. For instance, if a thirty-five-year-old surgeon were to lose the use of his or her hands, that individual would receive guaranteed income for the next thirty years.

Disability Insurance and Your Business

Depending on whether you are a business owner or an employee, you may consider different aspects of disability insurance.

If you are a business owner, you need to think about Business Overhead Expense (BOE) disability insurance. Let's say that your business is entirely dependent on you to pay for its overhead. That includes everything from rent to fixed expenses to salaries for your employees. In that case, you would want to look at a disability policy that would pay not only for the individual income you bring in, but for all of those other business expenses as well. You would no longer be personally liable for them. BOE policies are flexible and can be taken out for as many years as you need.

Disability policies can also be put to good use when it comes to business partners. For instance, say you had an arrangement between yourself and a business partner that if you were to die, your partner would buy out your spouse's interest in the business. That is a fairly typical agreement. But what a lot of people overlook is, what if you don't die? What if you only become disabled? Your partner might not have the lump sum available to buy out your interest right then and there. In that situation, if you had the right disability policy, your coverage would give your partner the funds he or she needed to buy you out. The disability insurance basically gives you the ability to fund that portion of your responsibility to your partner in this scenario.

If you are an employee or a business owner, the thing to remember is that, if possible, you never want your company to pay the premium on your disability insurance for you. That's because in the event that you ever need to claim disability, you will receive more income if you've been paying your premiums personally. Corporations will often offer to pay the premiums on their employees' disability policies because they get a tax write-off for doing so.

The downside is that when you as an individual claim disability, you end up paying taxes on it. On the other hand, if you have been paying your premiums yourself, the income you receive from your disability insurance is not taxable. Depending on your income bracket, your net result could be almost twice as much as it would have been if you had to pay the tax.

Disability insurance can be used in many different areas depending on how you want to structure your risk transfer. I usually advise my clients to start at the top and work their way down: first insure yourself, then insure your business, and finally insure your partner. That way, if something happens, you will know exactly where you stand.

Gap Elimination Checklist

Use the following checklist to begin The Gap Elimination Process™ for disability insurance.

✓ **Benefit Period**: The benefit period that disability insurance is typically purchased for is a fixed number of years (usually two, five, or ten years) or until a fixed age is reached (usually sixty-five, sixty-seven, or seventy).

✓ **Benefit Update (Future Purchase Option)**: This allows the client to increase the maximum monthly benefit amount without providing evidence of medical insurability. Typically, the client shows financial justification, such as a rise in income, to increase the benefit. The premium is adjusted based on current pricing and the client's current age. Benefit update is often called "future purchase option." An additional premium may be charged to give the client the option of increasing his or her benefits in the future.

✓ **Capital Sum Benefit**: This provides a one-time lump-sum benefit to help you adjust financially if there is a total loss of use, without the possibility of recovery, of: sight in at least one eye, a hand, or a foot. The capital sum benefit is typically payable in addition to any other benefits paid out by the policy.

✓ **Catastrophic Rider**: This coverage is thought of as "the LTC rider." It provides an additional monthly benefit if the client needs assistance with two of the six ADLs (bathing, continence, dressing, eating, toileting, and transferring) or if there is a cognitive issue such as Alzheimer's disease.

✓ **Cost of Living Adjustment (COLA)**: While you are disabled, your benefit is adjusted year after year by the COLA factor to help keep pace with inflation.

✓ **Elimination Period (EP)**: The EP is like a deductible. It is the period of time during which you are disabled and not receiving a benefit from the carrier. This period typically lasts 30, 60, 90, 180, or 365 days.

✓ **Future Benefit Increase Rider**: This automatically increases your coverage every year without evidence of insurability for what is typically a six-year period, based on the change in the Consumer Price Index (CPI).

✓ **Guaranteed Renewable**: Your carrier is required to continue your coverage as long as your premiums are paid, but it reserves the right to change your premiums based on an entire occupation class. Annual rates on a disability typically do not increase as you get older, but a carrier can raise your rate, provided it raises rates for everyone with the same occupation and plan type. In other words, you can't be singled out for a rate increase.

✓ **Maximum Monthly Benefit**: This is the total monthly benefit available to you from your base disability insurance plan

✓ **Non-Cancelable (Non-Can)**: Your premiums and your policy are non-cancelable, meaning that your carrier does not have the ability to alter either one of them.

✓ **Presumptive Disability Rider**: Regardless of whether the client is defined as disabled or not, this benefit pays a monthly benefit to the client if there is a permanent loss of the power of speech, hearing in both ears, sight in both eyes, or use of both hands, both feet, or one hand and one foot. Benefits are often extended to pay for life if the original benefit period selected was until age sixty-five or longer, depending on the carrier.

✓ **Residual Disability Rider**: If you are not totally disabled and are working in a new occupation as a result of sickness or injury that pays less than 80 percent of what you were earning in your previous occupation, this rider provides you with a portion of your policy's maximum monthly benefit.

✓ **Social Security Benefit Rider**: Most white-collar plans are not integrated with Social Security. However, if your plan includes this rider, it means that a portion of your monthly benefit is only payable when you do not receive a proportionate benefit from Social Security, workers' compensation, or Railroad Retirement. If the client receives benefits under one of these programs, the Social Security benefit rider will be reduced proportionately.

Chapter 8

Flood and Earthquake Insurance

Only after disaster can we be resurrected.

—CHUCK PALAHNIUK

The 1994 Northridge Quake

On January 17, 1994, I walked into my office to find it destroyed. File cabinets were overturned. Computers were on the floor. It looked as though gravity had taken a short vacation and come back without warning. Hours earlier, a 6.7-magnitude earthquake had struck twenty miles north of the office, at Northridge in California's San Fernando Valley. I took in the damage for a minute and then started cleaning up.

I had barely made a dent before my phone started ringing off the hook. My colleagues and I only had the time to take down names and addresses. Later that afternoon, we started visiting those on our lists.

The destruction was astounding. Some homes had moved off their foundations and were resting ten feet away in the middle of the family flower beds—a surreal sight because houses around them looked completely unscathed. I visited dozens of homes that day, and the damage ranged from very light to total demolition. Meanwhile, along the Interstate 10 freeway, bridges had collapsed and apartment complexes had flattened, trapping sleeping residents.

The Northridge quake claimed fifty-seven lives, injured 8,700 people, and amounted to $20 billion in damages, making it one of the costliest natural disasters in the history of the United States.

The Basics of Earthquake Insurance

The Northridge quake was big. But it wasn't as devastating as those in other countries. In 2005, an 8.6-magnitude quake killed 1,300 in Sumatra, Indonesia. In 2010, an 8.8-magnitude quake caused billions of dollars of damage in Chile. In 2011, a 9.0-magnitude undersea earthquake off the coast of Japan triggered tsunami waves that left a death toll of more than 15,000.

Many people don't realize that their regular homeowners insurance does not include any coverage for earthquakes. If you lose your home in a fire, your carrier will pay to reconstruct it up to the agreed-upon limits and cover your living expenses during the rebuilding. If, however, you lose your home in an earthquake, you are on your own. The only exception would be if the earthquake caused a fire, in which case your house would be covered for fire damage—and nothing else.

In California and other earthquake-prone states, people should seriously consider an earthquake policy. New fault lines are discovered all the time. These natural disasters are extremely unpredictable. However, serious quakes don't happen frequently or relatively regularly, so residents of risk-prone areas tend to overlook this coverage. It boils down to "out of sight, out of mind." Natural disasters are enormous "elephants" that happen suddenly and unexpectedly.

With earthquake insurance—as with all other kinds of insurance—foresight is key. No one thinks about the possibility of "the big one" until small quakes start rattling things around. When that happens, my phone rings constantly for a day or two with requests for earthquake insurance. But when a minor quake happens, all carriers put a temporary moratorium on selling quake insurance for two, three, or sometimes even four weeks. All I can do is collect names and offer to call people back.

When the moratorium lifts and I return the calls, however, many people have forgotten the seriousness of the threat and are no longer interested in coverage. Earthquake coverage has to be purchased before you need it, because after the fact it's too late.

Earthquake insurance is harder to navigate than most other types of coverage. Because of the unpredictability of earthquakes, deductibles for this policy tend to be high—typically about 10 or 15 percent. Moreover, the deductible is based on the amount of coverage you purchase, not the amount of your claim.

For instance, imagine you buy a $500,000 earthquake policy with a 15 percent deductible, and then a quake causes $20,000 of damage to your home. Your deductible would not be 15 percent of $20,000. It would be 15 percent of the $500,000 policy amount, which works out to $75,000. So you would not receive any compensation from your carrier to cover your $20,000 of home repairs.

The good news is that several carriers offer earthquake coverage. Because there's competition, your broker should be able to give you a few options to protect your assets from earthquake exposure. Ask about all the stand-alone carriers that write earthquake coverage, and compare them to what your home insurance carrier provides. Stand-alone carriers can, at times, have broader coverage and higher limits than an organization, such as the California Earthquake Authority (CEA). Consider all your options.

Earthquake coverage is not required by most lenders, so that means that most people who purchase it are "believers." They may have lived through the San Francisco or Northridge earthquakes and felt firsthand the tremendous destruction that can be unleashed in a few seconds. Alternately, they may have learned from other people's mistakes, having heard stories of the uninsured grappling with the aftermath of a major quake.

Even in Southern California, where we could have a major earthquake at any time, only a little over half of my clients choose to purchase this coverage. I always remind my clients that their homeowners policy provides no quake coverage and ask if they are okay with having zero earthquake protection. They are 100 percent self-insured, with no risk transfer. Sometimes that's what they want, but at least they know it's available and understand what they stand to lose.

The Basics of Flood Insurance

If you live in a flood zone and have a lender, you will have to purchase flood insurance.

The National Flood Insurance Program defines a flood as:

> *A general and temporary condition for partial or complete inundation of two or more acres of normally dry land area, or of two or more properties (at least one of which is your property) from: a) overflow of inland or tidal waters; b) unusual and rapid accumulation or runoff of surface waters from any source; or c) mudflow. Collapse or subsidence of land along the*

shore of a lake or similar body of water as a result of erosion or undermining caused by waves or currents of water exceeding anticipated cyclical levels that result in a flood.

Flood insurance premiums in many parts of the country are going up. That's because massive floods across the nation in recent years have resulted in huge claims and incredible destruction. Insurance pricing is based on maintaining strong reserves to pay for estimated claims. Recently, the flood insurance mapping program was updated to reflect expected claims. After that, coverage prices rose in almost every area of the country that has the potential to flood.

The maximum amount of coverage available with a primary flood insurance policy is $100,000 for contents (the possessions within your house) and $250,000 for building (meaning the house itself). In order to get additional coverage, you have to buy an excess flood policy. Some carriers sell excess flood coverage together with home insurance, provided you already have the primary policy. Other carriers, such as Lloyd's of London, offer stand-alone excess flood policies. In either case, the primary policy is still required.

If you buy a home that needs flood insurance, one way to minimize your cost is if the current owner already has flood insurance on the house. You may be able to take over or "grandfather" the pre-existing policy and, typically, pay less than if you were purchasing a brand new policy for the same house. Another way to reduce your premium is by increasing your deductible. In some cases, a higher deductible makes a lot of sense. Ask your broker for all possible deductible options before you decide on a plan.

Weigh and Balance Coverage

Earthquake insurance doesn't have many bells and whistles. You get a certain amount of coverage for dwelling and contents that is clearly spelled out. If it's not enough, there's no Extended Replacement Cost (ERC) endorsement like in a homeowners policy. Other endorsements, such as building ordinance, will also be limited, and the deductible for earthquake insurance is often large.

I'm not trying to make a case against purchasing earthquake insurance. Having some coverage is better than no coverage, especially if you live in an earthquake-prone area. However, it's important to know the details of your coverage up front so that there won't be surprises later.

Flood insurance is similar to earthquake: your home policy provides no such coverage. As with earthquake coverage, having something is better than nothing in the event of a flood. If the 100/250 (in thousands) limits of a basic policy are too low, you may need to buy an excess policy. You can buy as much or as little flood insurance as you like.

Neither earthquake nor flood coverage is designed to provide complete risk transfer and make you 100 percent whole after a disaster, as a home insurance policy might do. They will, however, go a long way toward putting your life back together in the aftermath of a violent earthquake or storm.

Gap Elimination Checklist for Earthquake

Use the following checklist to begin The Gap Elimination Process™ for earthquake insurance.

✓ **Building Code Upgrade Coverage**: This additional coverage provides funds to bring your home up to current building codes in the event of repair or replacement.

✓ **Building Property**: This coverage takes care of the repair or replacement of the structure when earthquake damage exceeds the deductible. Property covered includes built-in appliances, fixtures, some improvements, wall-to-wall carpeting, and other items.

✓ **Deductible**: The deductible for building and contents is based on the amount of coverage you have, not the amount of loss. For example, say you have a 15 percent deductible. If your coverage amount is $500,000 and your loss is $100,000, the carrier doesn't deduct the 15 percent deductible on the $100,000, but on the $500,000, which works out to be $75,000. So the amount of damage you would be paid for is $25,000.

✓ **Emergency Repairs**: This covers reasonable emergency repairs following an earthquake. Examples of "reasonable" repairs would be repair or replacement of covered broken windows in the dwelling and protection against further damage to covered property.

✓ **Loss Assessment**: This provides coverage for certain assessments that an association may impose on all property owners to pay for structural repairs resulting from earthquake damage when the damage exceeds the deductible, up to the policy limit.

✓ **Loss of Use**: If you are unable to live in your home as a result of earthquake damage, loss of use provides coverage for additional living expenses so you can rent temporary housing, up to the policy limit. Some policies, such as those from the California Earthquake Authority, do not have a deductible for loss of use.

✓ **Personal Property:** This coverage replaces personal property such as furniture, clothing, and household items when damage exceeds the coverage deductible, up to the policy limit.

Gap Elimination Checklist for Flood

Use the following checklist to begin The Gap Elimination Process™ for flood insurance. A flood insurance policy typically doesn't have optional coverage choices. You choose contents up to $100,000, building up to $250,000, and your deductible. This checklist provides definitions of policy terms for flood insurance.

✓ **Actual Cash Value (ACV):** This is the cost to replace an insured item of property at the time of loss, less the value of physical depreciation.

✓ **Base Flood:** This means a flood has a 1 percent chance of being equaled or exceeded in any given year.

✓ **Base Flood Elevation (BFE):** This is the level of floodwater expected to occur once in a hundred years. Generally, when constructing in the floodplain, this is the elevation that the lowest floor of the structure, including basements and crawlspaces, must remain at least one foot above.

✓ **Basement:** This refers to any area of the building, including any sunken room or sunken portion of a room, having its floor below ground level (subgrade) on all sides.

✓ **Breakaway Wall:** This wall is not part of the structural support of the building and is intended through its design and construction to collapse under specific lateral loading forces, without causing damage to the elevated portion of the building or supporting foundation system.

✓ **Community:** This is a political entity that has the authority to adopt and enforce floodplain ordinances for the area under its jurisdiction. In most cases, a community is an incorporated city, town, township, borough, village, or an unincorporated area of a county or parish. However, some states have statutory authorities that vary from this description.

✓ **Community Rating System (CRS):** This is a program developed by the Federal Emergency Management Agency (FEMA) Mitigation Division to provide incentives for communities in the National Flood Insurance Program that have gone beyond the minimum floodplain management requirements to develop extra measures to provide protection from flooding.

✓ **Deductible:** Flood policies have many deductible options—typically 500, 1,000, 2,500, and 5,000. Look into higher deductibles to reduce your premium.

✓ **Elevated Building:** This is a building that has no basement and has its lowest elevated floor raised above ground level by foundation walls, shear walls, posts, piers, pilings, or columns. Solid foundation perimeter walls are not an acceptable means of elevating buildings in certain zones (V and VE).

✓ **Elevation Certificate:** This certificate verifies the elevation data of a structure on a given property relative to the ground level. The certificate is used by local communities and builders to ensure compliance with local floodplain management ordinances and used by insurance agents and companies in the rating of flood insurance policies.

✓ **Enclosure:** This is the portion of an elevated building below the lowest elevated floor that is either partially or fully shut in by rigid walls.

✓ **Excess Coverage**: Some carriers will write limits above the basic flood policy. If your property has potential for large flood loss, look into an excess flood policy.

✓ **Federal Policy Fee:** This is a flat charge that the policyholder must pay on each new or renewal policy to defray certain administrative expenses incurred in carrying out the National Flood Insurance Program.

✓ **Flood:** This refers to a general and temporary condition of partial or complete inundation of two or more acres of normally dry land area or of two or more properties (at least one of which is the policyholder's property) from one of the following:

☐ Overflow of inland or tidal waters

☐ Unusual and rapid accumulation or runoff of surface waters from any source

☐ Mudflow

☐ Collapse or subsidence of land along the shore of a lake or similar body of water as a result of erosion or undermining caused by waves or currents of water exceeding anticipated cyclical levels that result in a flood as defined above

✓ **Flood Disaster Protection Act (FDPA) of 1973:** This law made the purchase of flood insurance mandatory for the protection of property located in Special Flood Hazard Areas.

✓ **Flood Hazard Boundary Map (FHBM):** This is an official map of a community issued by the Federal Insurance Administrator, where the boundaries of the flood, mudflow, and related erosion areas having special hazards have been designated.

✓ **Flood Insurance Rate Map (FIRM):** This is an official map of a community on which the Mitigation Division Administrator has delineated the special hazard areas and the risk premium zones applicable to the community.

✓ **Flood Zone (Zone):** This is a geographical area shown on an FHBM or FIRM that reflects the severity or type of flooding in the area.

✓ **Floodplain:** This is a land area susceptible to being inundated by floodwaters from any source.

✓ **Floodplain Management:** This is the operation of an overall program of corrective and preventive measures for reducing flood damage, including but not limited to emergency preparedness plans, flood control works, and floodplain management regulations.

✓ **Increased Cost of Compliance (ICC):** This is coverage for expenses a property owner must incur, above and beyond the cost to repair the physical damage the structure actually sustained from a flooding event, to comply with mitigation requirements of state or local floodplain management ordinances or laws.

Acceptable mitigation measures are elevation, flood-proofing, relocation, demolition, or any combination thereof.

✓ **Lowest Floor:** This refers to the lowest floor of the lowest enclosed area (including a basement). An unfinished or flood-resistant enclosure, usable solely for the parking of vehicles, building access, or storage in an area other than a basement area, is not considered a building's lowest floor provided that the enclosure is not built so as to render the structure in violation of requirements.

✓ **Mandatory Purchase:** Under the provisions of the FDPA of 1973, individuals, businesses, and others buying, building, or improving property located in identified areas of special flood hazards within participating communities are required to purchase flood insurance as a prerequisite for receiving any type of direct or indirect federal financial assistance (e.g., any loan, grant, guaranty, insurance, payment, subsidy, or disaster assistance) when the building or personal property is the subject of or security for such assistance.

✓ **Maximum Amount:** The maximum amount on a basic flood policy is $250,000 for buildings and $100,000 for contents. In most cases, you'll need at least this amount.

✓ **National Flood Insurance Program (NFIP):** This federal program enables property owners in participating communities to purchase insurance protection against losses from flooding. This insurance is designed to provide an insurance alternative to disaster assistance to meet the escalating costs of repairing damage to buildings and their contents caused by floods.

✓ **Non-Residential:** This includes but is not limited to small-business concerns, churches, schools, farm buildings, pool houses, clubhouses, recreational buildings, mercantile structures, agricultural and industrial structures, warehouses, hotels and motels with normal room rentals for less than six months' duration, and nursing homes.

✓ **Non-Special Flood Hazard Area (NSFHA):** This is an area in a low- to moderate-risk flood zone (Zones B, C, X) that is not in any immediate danger from flooding caused by overflowing rivers or hard rains. However, it's important to note that structures within a NSFHA are still at risk.

✓ **Other Residential:** These include hotels and motels where the normal occupancy of a guest is six months or more; a tourist home or rooming house that has more than four rooms; and a residential building (excluding hotels and motels with normal room rentals for less than six months' duration) containing more than four dwelling units. Incidental occupancies such as office, professional private school, or studio occupancy are permitted if the total area of such incidental occupancies is limited to less than 25 percent of the total floor area within the building.

✓ **Participating Community:** This is a community for which the Mitigation Division Administrator has authorized the sale of flood insurance under the NFIP.

✓ **Policy:** This is the entire written contract between the insured and the insurer. It includes the printed policy form, the application and declarations page, any endorsement(s) that may be issued, and any renewal certificate indicating that coverage has been instituted for a new policy and new policy term.

✓ **Post-FIRM Building:** This is a building for which construction or substantial improvement occurred after December 31, 1974, or on or after the effective date of an initial FIRM, whichever is later.

✓ **Pre-FIRM Building:** This is a building for which construction or substantial improvement occurred on or before December 31, 1974, or before the effective date of an initial FIRM.

✓ **Preferred Risk Policy (PRP):** This policy offers fixed combinations of building/contents coverage or contents-only coverage at modest, fixed premiums. The PRP is only available for properties located in certain zones (B, C, and X zones in regular program communities that meet eligibility requirements based on the property's flood-loss history).

✓ **Probation Surcharge (Premium):** This is a flat charge that the policyholder must pay on each new or renewal policy issued covering property in a community that the NFIP has placed on probation under the provisions of 44 CFR 59.24.

✓ **Replacement Cost Value (RCV):** This is the cost to replace property with the same kind of material and construction without deduction for depreciation.

✓ **Residential Condominium Building Association Policy (RCBAP):** This policy is issued to insure a residential condominium building and all units within the building, provided that the building is located in a Regular Program Community and at least 75 percent of the total floor area is residential.

✓ **Special Flood Hazard Area (SFHA):** This is a FEMA-identified high-risk flood area where flood insurance is mandatory for properties.

✓ **Standard Flood Insurance Policy (SFIP):** This policy is issued to insure a building and/or its contents.

✓ **Waiting Period:** This refers to the time between the date of application and the policy effective date. When buying a flood policy, there is a thirty-day waiting period unless your lender requires coverage. If flood damage occurs during the waiting period, there is no coverage.

✓ **Wave Height Adjustment:** This measurement is added to the base flood elevation for V Zones shown on the FIRM published before 1981. For coastal communities, the base flood elevation shown on FIRMs published before 1981 are still-water elevations, which include only the effects of tide and storm surges, and not the height of wind-generated waves.

✓ **Zone:** This is a geographical area shown on a FHBM or FIRM that reflects the severity or type of flooding in the area.

Chapter 9

Valuables and Collectibles
(Scheduled Items)

*There is only one success—to be able to
spend your life in your own way.*

—CHRISTOPHER MORLEY

The Exotic Meat Collection

Over the years, some unusual claims have come across my desk. One of the strangest was from a client who collected exotic canned meats. This man had some of the most bizarre meats you can imagine—possum, rattlesnake, you name it. Then one day, it was all stolen.

Most insurance companies have a list of valuables and collectibles called "target items" covered up to a limited amount in a regular homeowners policy. These include jewelry, fine art, rare comic books, and antique cars. Generally, anything unusual and expensive is specifically stated on this list, and everything else is covered by the regular policy.

The exotic canned meat collection was worth quite a bit of money. But no one had thought of putting "exotic canned meats" on the target items list. My client therefore argued that his regular homeowners policy should cover the loss.

He had a valid point. If there isn't a specifically noted limitation on your policy for any given item, then the policy is supposed to cover it. That means that if somebody steals your shoes, the carrier has to pay you what your shoes were worth. The same was true, my client made the case, for his meat collection.

We went back and forth with the carrier to determine the value of those exotic canned meats. My client's inventory was pretty sophisticated and turned out to be worth about $30,000. Eventually, the claim was approved by the carrier. The moral of this story? If your policy will allow you to schedule items, do it. That way, in the event of loss, the claim will be straightforward.

Your exotic items may be completely different than canned meats. But if you do not have the right insurance coverage, the experience will become a huge "elephant" for you.

The Basics of Scheduled Items

Every homeowners policy includes a fixed amount of coverage for personal items, such as furnishings, clothing, electronics, and so on. Because of this, many people mistakenly assume that their more valuable items—such as expensive jewelry and rare collections—are covered by their regular policy. Each carrier has a list of target items that are not covered past a certain amount under a standard insurance package. If you want complete coverage for any of these pricey possessions, you need to purchase it separately. This type of coverage is called "scheduled items."

Just about anything valuable that you collect—whether coins, stamps, or comic books—falls under scheduled items. The term arises from literally having to make a separate list—or schedule—of the items you want to insure that are not included in your basic homeowners policy. A schedule includes the item name, its description, and exactly how much it is worth. That way, if it needs to be replaced, you'll know in advance how much money you can expect to receive from your insurance provider.

When you purchase insurance for a scheduled item, you typically get all risk-transfer. This means that you receive compensation for the lost or damaged item regardless of why it was lost or damaged. It doesn't matter if it was a theft, fire, mysterious disappearance (with the right endorsement), or earthquake. Even if you just look down at the ring on your hand one day and realize, "Oh my goodness, the diamond is missing!" you will be covered by your carrier for the amount listed on your schedule.

The value of scheduled items is determined by appraisals. Every scheduled item you want to insure must be appraised, and those appraisals must be submitted before the items can appear on your scheduled items list. The objective is to establish the value of the collection or article in advance so that you don't have to worry about reconstructing its value after the fact. In the case of my exotic meats client, for example, having a valid appraisal of his collection saved him the frustration of trying to determine the true worth of his claim.

Keep in mind a couple of things when purchasing insurance for scheduled items. The first is the option of putting a stated value endorsement on your policy. A stated value endorsement guarantees that the carrier will give you the money for your lost or damaged item, as opposed to replacing it for you.

Imagine you have a one-carat diamond ring. The description on your scheduled items list will specify its size, cut, clarity, and color.

Unless you have a stated value policy on that ring, your carrier is allowed to send you another diamond that is purchased wherever it can get the best deal, as long as it technically has the same rating. You will not be personally involved in choosing a replacement that resonates with you. With a stated value endorsement, your carrier has the option to send you a check for the amount stated on your scheduled items policy, and you can to do whatever you want with that check.

Another thing to consider when insuring scheduled items is an extended replacement cost (ERC) endorsement. This means that if the market value of your scheduled item has gone up between when you purchased it and when you need it replaced, your policy will cover a percentage of that difference.

For example, when a client of mine was on vacation, he left his Rolex watch on the bedside table in his room for an hour or two while he went for a swim in the hotel pool. When he came back, it was gone. The watch was insured as a scheduled item for $40,000, which was his purchase cost. However, the price had gone up since then, and the cost to replace it was $48,000. Fortunately, my client had a 50 percent ERC endorsement on the watch. He received a check for the full $48,000 plus tax, which he used to buy a new Rolex that he no longer leaves in hotel rooms.

Schedule Your Jewelry

People don't always think about insuring their jewelry specifically, and this can end up being a costly mistake. My own family had to learn this lesson the hard way. My wife's grandfather was a successful jeweler, so her grandmother had a pretty spectacular collection of jewelry.

One day, two men robbed her while she was carrying her bags from the local shopping center to her car. They took all her jewelry—probably $250,000 worth of diamonds that she had accumulated over the years, marking the big milestones in her life. Unfortunately, there was no insurance coverage on them; otherwise my wife and her three sisters might have had some treasured family heirlooms in remembrance of their grandmother.

Just about every carrier has very small policy limits for jewelry. If the piece is destroyed in a fire, it will usually be fully covered. However, if anything else happens to it, the owner will generally receive a minimal amount of compensation. This is determined by the limits of the personal property clause of your homeowners insurance policy. Jewelry that is worth beyond those limits needs to be insured as a scheduled item.

A client of mine once had a beautiful gold Cartier watch. One night she wore it to a restaurant, and it became uncomfortable on her wrist, so she took it off and set it on the table. After dinner, she and her husband paid the check and left without a second thought. They were driving home when she realized that she had forgotten the watch. Of course, they turned around and hightailed it back there, but the watch was gone. Nobody ever found it. Luckily, the watch was insured for $35,000 plus a 50 percent ERC endorsement. She got exactly what she needed to buy a brand new one.

Schedule Your Art

The same process applies to scheduling art. Scheduling art is much less expensive than scheduling jewelry, because there is less risk involved. Your art doesn't travel with you or get left on restaurant tables. Therefore, the rates to schedule artwork are very reasonable.

An all-risk endorsement on art will cover nearly any scenario—fire, theft, earthquake, flood, wind, you name it. In the case of a natural disaster, your artwork might be the only thing that you can safely get coverage for. Unlike a regular personal property endorsement in a homeowners policy, which wouldn't be triggered by a flood or earthquake, scheduled items are protected against natural disasters as much as they are against anything else.

If you are fortunate enough to have a large schedule of artwork, your carrier may actually provide concierge-type services to transport and store your collection. An agent I know had a client whose scheduled art was worth hundreds of millions of dollars. The client lived in Los Angeles and wanted to display his collection at a museum in New York. When the carrier learned about this, it put together a security detail at its own expense to escort the art across the country.

The detail included armed guards posted both in the front and back of the truck carrying the art collection. Every hour, one of the guards had to check in with a representative at the insurance company to let him know exactly how things were going. Because the schedule was so valuable to the carrier, it handled everything and footed the bill. The client never would have known about that service on his own. A conversation with his agent and carrier provided all the services he needed for his prized art collection to make a safe trip.

Other Scheduled Items

Scheduled items can vary widely. Nowadays, more and more individuals schedule their wine collections. These can be worth a significant amount, and by scheduling their collections, the owners insure the wine against faulty storage, breakage, earthquakes, and the like. Even if the wine evaporates through the cork and the amount of liquid in the bottle drops to a certain level, some carriers will cover it.

Classic car collections are another frequently scheduled item. Depending on the number of cars and their value, consider scheduling them. If you don't drive them much, it doesn't make sense to pay all the costs typically involved in insuring a car. In that case, a carrier can insure your cars as collectibles, and that rate is very good. With car collections you can get agreed value coverage, meaning that your carrier gives you insurance for the appraised value of the collection. A good carrier will let you dictate the choice of body shops you can use if the cars are damaged. Some carriers specialize in this kind of coverage.

One client of mine had an incredible comic book collection. He had been working on it for thirty years, and had managed to fill seven or eight giant trunks—the kind that people used to travel with in the 1920s and 1930s—with collector-grade comics. All he did on weekends was go to comic book shows; it was his passion. Other people collect unique things, like antique vases. There's no end to the fascinating collections people have, and almost all of them fall under scheduled items when it comes to insurance.

Gap Elimination Checklist

Use the following checklist to begin The Gap Elimination Process™ for scheduled items.

Coverage details include:

✓ **Breakage Coverage for Fine Arts:** Fine arts can be divided into two categories: fragile and non-fragile. Any item that is listed as fragile will be covered in the event of breakage, with this endorsement.

✓ **High-Deductible Options:** Scheduled floater polices can have the option of giving you a deductible before coverage begins. The higher the deductible, the lower the premium.

✓ **Agreed Value:** Items insured at agreed value typically require an appraisal in order to be scheduled. The appraised value will be shown on the schedule. In the event of loss, the agreed amount is what you'll receive. Whenever possible, get an agreed value endorsement.

✓ **Extended Replacement Cost** (ERC): The ERC endorsement will pay an additional percentage above and beyond the agreed value if the insured item appreciates. For example, suppose a ring scheduled for $10,000 is stolen. At time of loss, the current replacement cost is found to be $13,000. If you had a 50 percent ERC endorsement, you would be able to collect up to $15,000. The carrier would pay the $13,000 needed to replace the ring.

✓ **Optional Earthquake Coverage:** Some personal article floater policies will exclude earthquake coverage depending on where the article is physically stored. Make sure that your article floater policy includes earthquake coverage, especially for your fragile/breakable items.

✓ **Scheduled or Blanket Coverage:** Items in a personal article floater policy can be scheduled or "blanketed." Scheduled items are appraised and the amount of coverage is listed for each item. For example, if an engagement ring is appraised at $25,000, then the scheduled ring would be listed for $25,000 worth of coverage in the policy.

✓ **Blanket Coverage:** Blanket coverage means that all items within the blanket are covered together for one combined amount. There is usually a limit per item within blanket coverage. For example, the policy might cover $100,000 total for fine arts or jewelry, but there could be a maximum coverage limit of $20,000 for any one item within the group.

Consider scheduled items if you have any:

✓ **Cameras:** This includes cameras, lenses, flash equipment, and accessories for personal use.

✓ **Fine Art:** This includes artwork, antique furniture, oriental rugs, and antique musical instruments or guns used solely for display.

✓ **Furs:** This includes garments made of or trimmed with natural fur.

✓ **Guns:** This includes legally owned firearms, scopes, cases, and accessories.

✓ **Jewelry:** Scheduled jewelry could include items such as rings, necklaces, earrings, bracelets, and watches. You can insure an individual item up to the value you specify, or you can insure an entire jewelry collection.

✓ **Musical Instruments:** Musical instruments and their accessories that are owned for personal use can be covered in scheduled items.

✓ **Other Collections and Collectibles:** Examples that could be covered under this category include wine collections, collectibles, memorabilia, sports cards, collectible coins, collectible paper money, rare coins and currency, display books, stamp collections, stamp display books, and collection cabinetry.

✓ **Silverware:** Silverware includes flatware, pieces of tea and coffee serving sets, and candle holders made of or plated with silver, gold, or pewter.

Chapter 10

Choose a Helping Hand

Knowing is not enough; we must apply.
Willing is not enough; we must do.

—JOHANN WOLFGANG VON GOETHE

The Importance of Relationships

In any important area of your life, relationships are everything. Think about your relationship with your doctor, lawyer, CPA, or fitness instructor. In most cases, those are long-term relationships. You've built them up. You've invested time and money into them so that you'll be able to do business with them efficiently. You know that you can count on these people because, thanks to those strong relationships, you've established a solid level of trust with them.

The same thought process and the same type of relationship needs to be established with your insurance professional.

I can tell you from experience that having a strong relationship with my clients makes a huge difference. We work more efficiently and build that important level of trust. We make sure that we are on the same page. Then when something happens and they need me, that bond goes a long way toward making sure that I know exactly how to be there to help them get back on their feet. We are there to protect our clients from the proverbial elephant and from unexpected loss.

Small Agencies versus Large Agencies

Your agent is your first point of contact with your insurance coverage, and it's important to choose someone you can trust. However, your agent isn't the only factor you should consider before you sign up. You also need to make sure that you have a reliable agency and carrier.

When choosing an agency, it's important to know the direction in which the industry is headed. As of 2013, consolidation into larger agencies was the theme. This proved beneficial to consumers because larger agencies have larger staffs, which helps them to properly service accounts, and because carriers try to bring in as much premium as they can, which is a lot easier to do at larger agencies than at smaller ones. Consequently, smaller agencies—the one-man shops with minimal staff—are getting swept away under the changes.

Before you can build a long-term relationship with your insurance professional, you need to make sure that person's agency will be around for the long term. Find one that is a decent size and properly staffed. That way, you'll know you're on stable ground before you even get started.

Build a Relationship with Your Carrier

It's equally important to have a good relationship with your carrier. A lot of people don't realize that you can do this, but you can. Best of all, if you take the time to do it, it will almost certainly save you some money at the end of the day.

First and foremost, you stand to save a lot of money by having as many lines of business as you can with the same carrier. For example, if you insure two cars, it will be less expensive than if you insure just one car because you get a multicar discount. If you insure your house in addition to those two cars, you get another discount. If you insure your house, your cars, your life, and your umbrella coverage with the same carrier, you get additional savings.

Having a lot of multiline discounts often adds up to dramatic savings. In many cases, the costs can be as much as 20, 30, or even 40 percent lower than what you would have paid for those policies individually. You will also receive additional savings on things like life insurance and insurance for certain occupations. All told, consolidating with a carrier ends up earning you a considerable advantage. Try to make it a one-stop shop.

Another benefit to having a strong carrier relationship is that you become more valuable as a customer. Your consolidating with a carrier makes them want to do everything they can to keep you. Carriers are businesses, and every business is in the industry to make a profit. They know they will have claims. If possible, they want to keep the amount of claims they get to a minimum. Therefore, a short-term customer with a lot of claims who doesn't have a good relationship with the carrier may not get the same consideration as a long-term multiline client.

Let's say you have a really good relationship with your carrier. Let's say you're a long-term customer who has auto, home, umbrella, and several other types of coverage with the same carrier. You're a responsible person and don't file claims very often. In that scenario, you are a valuable customer. You are someone the carrier wants to keep.

So if you suddenly need to file a big claim, and your agent needs to persuade the carrier to keep you on, he or she will have a lot of ammunition. Your agent can make a strong case on your behalf because you've built a good relationship with that carrier over time. They say membership has its privileges, and the longer you've been with a carrier, the stronger the relationship will be. It definitely makes a difference.

Finally, just like every other aspect of insurance, it pays to follow up with carriers. Discounts come and go. Sometimes they fall through due to programming errors. Stay on top of any changes by having that regular review with your agent to make sure that you're always getting the best possible pricing.

Insure Your Life

Now you know the ropes. You've familiarized yourself with the broad categories of insurance. You've chosen an agency that is well staffed, and you've signed on with an accessible agent who you can trust. You've built a strong relationship with your carrier. You understand the basic principles of The Gap Elimination Process™, and you're committed to having regular reviews to keep up to date.

You have everything you need to insure your life.

Planning your insurance properly before a crisis happens should be part of everyone's philosophy. Take the steps that are right for you. Have a deeper dialogue with your agent. And build a secure fortress around your assets that no disaster will ever be able to destroy.

A full-service insurance agency should be able to help with all of the following policies:

✓ **Home insurance**

✓ **Scheduled items**

✓ Auto insurance

✓ Umbrella

✓ Rental/landlord insurance

✓ Earthquake insurance

✓ Flood insurance

✓ Long-term care/disability

✓ Life insurance

✓ Disability insurance

✓ Estate tax funding

✓ Annuities/IRAs

✓ Health insurance

✓ Business insurance

✓ Apartment building insurance

✓ Errors and omissions coverage

✓ Workers compensation

✓ Commercial real estate

Closing Thoughts

This book was written to help you learn about insurance and properly insure yourself and your family. I hope this book has helped you feel more knowledgeable about the world of insurance and how to secure your assets. This book gives you the tools to have an informed conversation with your insurance professional, so that you understand what is available and how it applies to you. Knowledge is power!

At the beginning of this book, I shared with you the story of an elephant sitting on a friend's husband. It is humorous, but it is also tragic. Life is filled with unexpected turns. While insurance cannot completely prevent unexpected events from happening, it can mitigate the risks and tragedy if they do.

I hope this book gives you the security and protection that you need, so that no matter where you go, no matter what happens to you—and even if an elephant sits on you—you and your family will be safe and covered.

You do not have to do this on your own. Once you decide what type of experience you prefer for yourself and your family, your insurance broker can help create and maintain the right plan. The final decision is ultimately yours. We are here to help you.

ᝣᝰᝤ

About the Author

Bart Baker is one of the most dependable insurance brokers in the western United States, as designated by Goldline Research. He has served on Farmers Insurance Group's President's Council since 2004 and is a Top of the Table qualifier of the Million Dollar Round Table (MDRT). LUTCF-designated, Baker is a highly sought-after speaker and trainer, and he was featured by Farmers in its national True Stories campaign.

Baker co-owns BW Baker Insurance Service with his wife of more than thirty-seven years, Wendy. As an L.A. County firefighter, Baker witnessed firsthand the devastation that can occur in people's lives without warning. Now retired from the fire department after twenty years of service, Baker continues to protect people and their assets by picking up where firefighting left off: with insurance.

Baker and Wendy built their business and raised their three children in Malibu, California, where they still reside. They are generous supporters of the Boys & Girls Clubs of America, as well as the Lighthouse for Women & Children shelter program.

෴

In reading this book, I hope that you have gained knowledge that will better prepare you for the future. I appreciate the time you've invested in furthering your insurance education.

I would like to give you a free gift of the Gap Elimination Checklist for homeowners insurance. Please go to www.readbartsbook.com, enter your email address where indicated, and a PDF of the checklist will be sent to you.

For more information

We welcome inquiries about your insurance needs.
Please contact us at:

B.W. Baker Insurance
www.bwbaker.com
29169 Heathercliff Road, Suite 208
Malibu, CA 90265
bart@bwbaker.com
(310) 457-5092

40726515R00079

Made in the USA
Lexington, KY
16 April 2015